CW00482637

STAIR

by

CHARLES DYER

SAMUEL FRENCH

LONDON
NEW YORK SYDNEY TORONTO HOLLYWOOD

STAIRCASE

First presented by the Royal Shakespeare Company (in association with Bill Freedman and Charles Kasher) at the Aldwych Theatre, London, on 2nd November 1966, with the following cast of characters:

CHARLES DYER, Paul Schofield

HARRY LEEDS, Patrick Magee

The play directed by PETER HALL
Setting by TIMOTHY O'BRIEN
Policeman's voice by ROGER LLOYD PACK

Subsequently presented at the Biltmore Theatre, Broadway, N.W., on 10th January 1968, with the following cast:

CHARLES DYER, Eli Wallach

HARRY LEEDS, Milo O'Shea

The play directed by BARRY MORSE

The action of the play takes place in a barber's shop called *Chez Harry*

ACT I

SCENE 1   Evening
SCENE 2   Half-an-hour later

ACT II

Early the next morning

Time—the present

THE SCENE

The scene is a Barber Shop called *Chez Harry*. The outside entrance is up C, and there is a door to the stock room up R. Between these doors can be seen the outline of the staircase belonging to the building. Under the recess formed by the staircase are shelves containing bottles of toilet preparations, etc. and a cash register. There is a large window L, with a customers' bench running below it. There are two barber's chairs, one RC (HARRY's CHAIR) and one LC (CHARLIE's CHAIR). Down R and down L are two basins, corresponding to the chairs, with mirrors above and cupboards beside them. Upstage of the L basin is a small table with an electric kettle and various pieces of crockery, and on shelves above are tins of tea, sugar, etc. There is a small stool down R, and a manicurist's table R of HARRY's CHAIR.

ACT I

This is the story of two middle-aged men.

When the CURTAIN *rises,* CHARLIE *is sitting in his barber's chair* LC, *a sheet tucked to his chin, and* HARRY *has just finished shaving him.* HARRY *wears a large bandage turban-wise about his head. Handel's 'Hallelujah Chorus' thunders from Harry's little portable record-player which is placed on the upstage end of the customer's bench.* HARRY *neatens Charlie's sideboard with a flourish of the razor, then moves to the stockroom door up* R. *He pops into the stock room for a moment, yelps, and returns, tossing a hot towel from hand to hand. This he pats on to Charlie's face.* HARRY *now removes his white jacket, which has "Harry" embroidered on its pocket, and hangs it on the stand up* LC. *He dons a cardigan, takes the sheet from Charlie, and tucks it round his own chin. He then sits in his chair,* RC. CHARLIE *rises, tosses his towel into the sink* L, *takes his white coat, with* "CHARLES" *on its pocket, and puts it on. He fetches another towel from the stock room, with a yelp, and plops it on Harry's face, leaving the stock-room door open when he re-enters from it. For a while he pats and slaps; and then he switches off the record player.*

CHARLIE. Funny day, Sunday.

(HARRY *mumbles through the hot towel*)

Ought to get that gas man in. That gas man. Only asking for trouble.

(HARRY *mumbles*)

Oh lovely. Lovely. What! Each time you open the door the flame goes puff.

HARRY. All nice and homely, dear.

CHARLIE. Oh witty! Witty! Let's hope you're laughing when they find us stiff and carbonized or whatever happens.

HARRY. Can you do that blackhead by my jawbone?

CHARLIE. Oh you are an obscene bag. Where's your culture? Sssh!

HARRY. What?

CHARLIE. There she goes!

(HARRY *rises, and they stand beneath the staircase up* R, *listening, like two little gnomes*)

HARRY. Nine p.m. dead on!

CHARLIE. Ssssh! Here she is!

(We hear clumping footsteps down the stairs. HARRY *and* CHARLIE *follow the noise down with their eyes)*

Here's the typing bit.

(A MAN *shouts in a loud voice off)*

MAN *(off)* Thank you, Miss Ricard. I'll collect the manuscript tomorrow.

HARRY. Doorbang!

(The door bangs)

CHARLIE. One, two, three, four, five . . .

HARRY. Sssh!

(The front door creaks. The footsteps creak up the stairs. Again CHARLIE *and* HARRY *follow the noise with their eyes. They end up, craning their necks at the ceiling. There is a faint thud above)*

CHARLIE. There's her left boot!

HARRY *(returning to his chair and sitting)* Oogh, I'll increase Miss Ricard's rent: that's a single bed-sitter.

CHARLIE *(moving* c*)* Double-thumper now, Harry. Where were we?

HARRY. Doing my bla–– pimple.

CHARLIE *(fetching some cottonwool from the shelves up* c*)* Oh yes. *(He prods and presses at Harry's face with lumps of cotton wool)*

HARRY. Filthy habit. Filthy. Reckon Nature's all to cock, I do.

CHARLIE. Nature! Nature! Can't blame Nature for Miss Ricard. What! Local camp bicycle, she is. Blame the Industrial Revolution.

HARRY. I meant everyone. Whole arrangement. Mortifies me, Charlie—biology does.

CHARLIE. Oh Doctor Harry Leeds, M.D.

HARRY. Don't mention doctors! People treating them like Jesus; humping around in stethoscopes, discussing functions in loud pompous voices.

CHARLIE. And who told that filthy joke about a lesbian in the powder room?

HARRY. Oh, not jokes, Charlie! Don't mind a gag, I don't; but I believe . . .

CHARLIE. Where's the surgical spirit?

HARRY. Um, I was topping up the shaving lotion—um, in my cupboard . . .

*(*CHARLIE *moves above Harry's chair to the cupboard* R, *takes out a bottle of surgical spirit, returns to* L *of Harry and dabs his face)*

It's just that I feel that Sex—all Sex could have been better arranged.

CHARLIE. You won't please rabbits with this, mate.

HARRY. Rabbits don't need to think. Don't suppose they even talk about it: *they* have nothing to talk *about*, don't you see?

CHARLIE. You what? You what! I should rub a dub!

HARRY. Oh, don't start arguing.

CHARLIE. Arguing! I reckon rabbits have nothing *else* to think about.

HARRY. Yes, but—what I mean—well, I think humans could have been made all the same.

CHARLIE. All men? No women, d'you mean?

HARRY. No, not completely. There'd have been sections of the community for feeding um, progeny and . . .

CHARLIE. Well! Get you for a communistic buttercup!

HARRY. I believe half Man's trouble's, due to Nature's reproductive systems, I do. I firmly believe this, Charlie. Oh, you can scoff. But it should be nicer, cleaner, *prettier*. It shouldn't be so folded up and sort of underneath.

CHARLIE. Juggling us about a bit, aren't you, dear! And where, pray, should we keep our paraphernalia? On our heads?

HARRY. And why not, *pray*! What's wrong with having, say, a couple of antennas. Males. Females. The lot. Nothing different or sniggery. Pleasant smile; raise your hat; shake antennas; good laugh in the bargain.

CHARLIE. Oh lovely, dear! Lovely! Just what I fancy in the morning—good laugh and shake me antennas. (*He returns the bottle to its cupboard, and moves* C)

(HARRY *rises, folds up his sheet, puts it on top of his cupboard, then throws his towel into the basin* R)

HARRY. There'd be no shame, I think. I think there'd be a kind of—picturesqueness about antennas on folk's heads. (*His lip quivers slightly*) I shouldn't be as I am if it had been an easy business—nice and clean and open.

CHARLIE. Starting our weeping stint, are we? Our weeping stint?

HARRY (*strongly*) No, we're not.

CHARLIE. Splendid! (*He sits in his chair* LC)

(HARRY *brings the manicurist's table to* R *of Charlie, then the stool, sits beside him and begins manicuring Charlie's nails*)

Antennas, she wants! Antennas.

HARRY. Oh, shut your mouth. Keep the draught out.

CHARLIE. You're including greyhounds and alligators in this system, I take it?

HARRY. All God's creatures.

CHARLIE. Poor old porcupine wouldn't know where to start.

HARRY. You don't care for anyone's feelings, you don't.

CHARLIE. I can just see crush hour—crush hour on the tube; pass down the car, raise your hat! Half the typing pool'd be on you for paternity.

HARRY. Oh no. Not at all. There'd be a method of folding them away during . . .

CHARLIE. Ha! Folding 'em up already! (*He jumps out of the chair, gleefully*)

HARRY. Ah no . . .

CHARLIE. Folding 'em, dear! Folding 'em, you said.

HARRY. You ridicule everyone's high principles, *you* do!

CHARLIE. So I should think, when they stick antennas on crocodiles! (*He sits back in the chair*)

(HARRY *continues the manicuring*)

(*After a while*) Started the old sulking stint, have we? Sulking stint?

HARRY. No.

CHARLIE. Because you ought to glory in God, you ought. What! Don't know what trouble is.

(HARRY *sings the "Hallelujah Chorus" under his breath*)

—Should be sitting where I am, mate; dreading what the post may bring. Try *that* on your bloody hallelujahs!

HARRY. You're safe enough. No post on Sundays.

CHARLIE. They could *deliver* it, couldn't they?

HARRY. Thought you'd decided it was too late.

CHARLIE. That was Ronnie Unsworth; not me. They're forced to send a Summons within forty-eight hours, Ronnie Unsworth said.

HARRY. Must be twelve days, now.

CHARLIE. Thirteen. Mind me quick! (*He snatches his hand away*)

(HARRY *rises and moves* L *to the window*)

HARRY. I don't know what it's all for; just don't understand. If I was asked if I'd like to die—peacefully and—and beautifully—right now, I reckon I'd acquiesce. D'you fancy an hour's television?

CHARLIE. Blood, bowels and bestiality. No thanks.

HARRY (*pressing his nose to the green curtains*) It's sort of wood-smokey outside; a night when your heels make chumf-chumfing noises as they bite the pavement. I can sense mist in the valleys; sheep coughing. Oh, church bells're so damn lonely.

CHARLIE. Sheep? Bells? We're backing on the gas works, mate.

HARRY. I was remembering young days; me and me sisters—used to run giggling to wash our faces in May dew.

CHARLIE. Coughing sheep and May dew! That was a quick winter.

(HARRY *moves to the stockroom door and closes it, then replaces the stool and manicurist's table* R)

Oh hell! (*He rubs his face*) If they'd only give me a sign. A sign. If they'd tell me it was cancelled, eh? Be such ecstasy, that would.

HARRY. Here! D'you fancy a bit of gardening?

CHARLIE. Middle of the night! On the mad stint, are we? Where, pray?

HARRY. In the yard.

CHARLIE. *Our* yard! They've written hymns about those satanic cobbles.

HARRY. There's Mum's seed boxes; switch on the stockroom light and it'd shine . . .

CHARLIE. No, no, no! Bluddyell—gardening! Grubby nails; earth worms snapping at your Wellingtons.

HARRY. Shall we go upstairs, then?

CHARLIE. *We? We?*

HARRY. What're *you* going to do, then?

CHARLIE. Stay in the shop. Lovely. I like it.

HARRY. There's nothing to do, Charlie.

CHARLIE. You what! There's mirrors to look in; swinging chairs; and all those pretty prophylactics to blow up. Lovely! (*He swings himself round in the chair*)

HARRY. We've got some marzipan roll from yesterday's elevenses; and I could do a little brew-up.

CHARLIE. Mm. All right. If you like. (*He takes a letter from his pocket and reads*)

(HARRY *moves down* L *and bustles with an electric kettle, filling it and plugging it in*)

HARRY. You know, last night I dreamt I was climbing a staircase. And I was naked except for a comb in me hair and a jock-strap.

CHARLIE. Well! Get "Bubbles".

HARRY. Thinking about holidays caused it. You know, we were saying how nice it'd be—tripping along some beach in a tiddly pair of briefs; people admiring our suntan. But we'd forgotten, Charlie; and last night I caught sight of myself in the bathroom mirror.

CHARLIE (*perusing his letter*) D'you think she'll expect me to collect her at the station tomorrow? Cassy?

HARRY (*taking some marzipan roll from the shelf and unwrapping it*) Anyhow, that'd be what caused the comb and jock-strap. 'Course, I knew it wasn't real—even in the dream. S'years since I woke up, clutching the quilt for shillin's. But I stepped out in this dream—stepped out and watched myself climb that staircase. It was horrible, Charlie. I saw a fat old man, bloated and hanging. I was flabby and ridiculous and I knew it. Paunch like a pig; freckled and grisly and . . .

CHARLIE. I'll be ill in a minute.

HARRY. Oh, you sardonic bitch! Easy for you: you've kept your looks. But I'm finished—even though I'm the same inside. I'm wearing tiddly briefs inside, Charlie, and my heart can still dance; but who knows it? Who'd want me on a beach? A yellowing sow's ear . . .

CHARLIE. Urgh, you're a messy talker! Walk tall! Walk tall!

(HARRY *puts tea in the pot*)

HARRY. I've given up expecting beneficence from you.

CHARLIE. Who're you kicking, eh? Who're you kicking? We're all depreciating, mate. What about my varicose veins? Varicose veins! Me legs're like fouled parrots' perches. Can hardly get my wind; and haven't seen me knee-caps since fifty-three. (*He swings out of his chair and moves* R)

HARRY. But you're still beautiful on the surface, Charlie.

CHARLIE (*considering himself in the mirror* R) Oh—I don't know.

HARRY. You are, Charlie. That's where you're lucky.

CHARLIE. I've kept myself in trim. Jowls wobble a bit.

HARRY. Doesn't show. (*He pours hot water into the pot*)

CHARLIE. What d'you reckon Cassy'll think?

HARRY. She should be very proud.

CHARLIE. I didn't mean it that way. I meant—I meant us.

HARRY (*looking up*) None of her business, is it?

CHARLIE (*nods*) Thought we might close early tomorrow.

HARRY. Oh?

CHARLIE. If you wouldn't mind, Harry. I mean—'s'only every twenty years, eh? Father seeing his daughter for the first time.

HARRY. Quarter of a century.

CHARLIE. Don't exaggerate. She's only twenty-one or two. Ooogh, the conniving sow. Robbed me of my youth, she did.

HARRY. Cassy?

CHARLIE. No, her mother: only married me for the sheer purpose of—of begetting, as they'd have it in the Bible.

HARRY. And I will put enmity between thy seed and her seed.

CHARLIE (*moving* LC) Eh? What's this, then?

HARRY. Somewhere in Genesis or Leviticus.

CHARLIE. On our religious stint, are we? Religious stint?

HARRY. Go on: I'm not stopping you talking.

CHARLIE. Forgotten where I was now.

HARRY. Grumbling, because you'd been a father: a privilege denied thousands of us.

CHARLIE. Privilege, was it! Oh, I should rub a dub, dear. What! Nine months of sick mornings, two bitchy weeks in Maternity—she flung me daffodils in a bedpan; and after an eternity of yowling, on me only silent night—there was a note pinned to the cot. Left me! They left me!

(HARRY *pours the tea*)

Even me honeymoon was a—a—a holocaust: one night of passion and food-poisoning for thirteen. Maggots in the haddock, she claimed.

(HARRY *giggles*)

Oh, I was laughing. Yes! What! Lovely—your blushing bride all shivering and turgid in the promenade shelter; hurricanes whipping the shingle. Couldn't even paddle for a plague of jellyfish.

(HARRY *roars with laughter. He gives Charlie his tea and leads him to his chair*)

HARRY. Come and have your tea, dear.

CHARLIE (*sitting in his chair*) She had years of allotments, you know. Fifty bob a week, Harry, fifty bob, it was.

HARRY. Must've been a nasty divorce judge.

CHARLIE. Nasty—he wore a black cap, dear! Divorce hearing— black cap! (*In a nasal voice*) "Oh, we're in the Theatre, are we," he said. 'Course I was big time in those days, Harry. Played all the Number Ones. Don't think you realize just how big I was.

HARRY. Yes I do. (*He fetches his own tea and sits in his chair* RC)

CHARLIE. Ask Archy Selder. Archy Selder'll tell you.

HARRY. Yes I know.

CHARLIE. Too true! But Theatre's a dirty word, see, Harry. Dirty word, it is. "Oh, we're in the Theatre, are we," he said, speaking on the verge of a burp. Well, I was young, see. Young, I was. And for a gag—a gag, that's all, Harry—I said: "We?" I said. "What pantomime are you in, then?"

HARRY. You never told me this.

CHARLIE. I didn't? Oh yes, dear. Brought the house down. Oogh, but the Judge went puce. Puce, he went. Bats fluttered from his ears. I reckon he doubled me allotment. *And* she got custody of the child. I was *robbed* of my child. Robbed! The most expensive joke *I* ever cracked.

HARRY. Oh—I can't see it. No. (*He shakes his head with indrawn breath*)

CHARLIE. What's the doubt, then?

HARRY. Doesn't sound like English fairness to me.

CHARLIE. Fairness! You're not crouching there believing in Justice, you ramshackle twit! There's no Justice, mate; and never will be till we have computers on the Bench; and then I'll get one that needs oiling.

(HARRY *still shakes his head*)

Look, stop shaking your head! (*Seeming strangely irritable*) What're you accusing me of, eh? Go on, say it!

HARRY. Say what?

CHARLIE. Oh belt up! (*He swings out of his chair and moves to the mirror* L. *He picks up the letter again and moves up* C, *perusing it*) *I* can't get Cassy into television, for heaven's sake.

HARRY. Must know someone she could meet.

CHARLIE. Who—the canteen manager? I've done one mingy commercial in ten years. Duffle coats. Sixteen guineas and four repeats. All I said was "Heave up the spinnaker!"

HARRY. Came over well.

CHARLIE. Yes; too well! This is the sow's *first* letter—except for that filthy postcard when I was late with her allotment; you know, when Mother had those vomiting spells. And just because I'm Networked wearing gumboots, yacht cap and royal blue bumfreezer, I'm wanted. Me daughter seeking fame. *And* Ronnie Unsworth's been sniffing around again.

HARRY (*rising and moving down* L) Marzipan roll? (*He hands the plate of cake to Charlie*)

CHARLIE. Ta. (*He takes a piece and moves above his chair*)

(HARRY *replaces the cake, takes a piece himself, and returns to his own chair*)

Oh, it would come now, wouldn't it just! Police hanging over my head and—d'you know I even had a begging card addressed to the Duffle Coat Man? "Are you aware of the many sick and needy mariners?" Haven't we any Eccles cake?

HARRY. You had it yesterday.

CHARLIE. Damn liar!

HARRY. I am not.

CHARLIE. Oh yes you are. Liar, mate!

HARRY. No, Charlie. *You* ate it whilst you were blow-waving that guitarist.

CHARLIE. Oh. (*He moves* L *and sits on the downstage end of the customers' bench*) So, er—will you be going out at all, then?

HARRY. Why?

CHARLIE. When Cassy comes.

HARRY. Why should I?

CHARLIE (*shrugging*) Well, she's my daughter.

HARRY. So?

CHARLIE. Nothing—nothing. (*He puts his marzipan roll on the bench beside him and picks up a magazine*) Er—I can borrow Ronnie Unsworth's car any time I like.

HARRY. Oh yes? Borrow his car?

CHARLES. Might be an idea if we took your mother for a spin.

HARRY. *We?*

CHARLIE. Mm. She's stuck in the attic up there, isn't she, poor thing. Do her good—bit of a blow.

HARRY. She's seized with arthritis, Charles; can't move. (*He cocks a suspicious eye at Charlie*)

CHARLIE. We could hoist her down the stairs; make a sort of—um—cradle.

HARRY. Energetic all of a sudden, aren't we? Why this interest in Mum? You haven't mentioned her name in ten years.

CHARLIE. I beg yours. I beg yours! Bought her that pot plant for Christmas.

HARRY. Who carried it upstairs?

CHARLIE. Paralyzed, are you?

HARRY. Couldn't go near Mother, you said. Her slippers ponged, you said.

CHARLIE. That's—um—why I thought we should give her a bit of a blow.

HARRY. You think I'm simple! "Give Mother a blow!"

CHARLIE. It's no more than I'd do for my own mother—except she's stuck in that place; and I *visit* her, you see.

HARRY. When?

CHARLIE. Every Saturday.

HARRY. I meant when does my mother get her blow?

CHARLIE. Um . . .

HARRY. Tomorrow evening?

CHARLIE. Good idea! Lovely!

HARRY. Cassy's coming.

CHARLIE. She is? Oh, good gracious!

HARRY. Yes.

CHARLIE. Harry! Take her yourself. Ronnie Unsworth wouldn't mind.

HARRY (*rising and facing Charlie*) Oogh, you send me right up the flue! Deceitful bitch! Hoist my mother down the landing! You'd as soon set fire to her drawers.

CHARLIE. Well, thank you, Vicar!

HARRY. I'm not one of your disc jockeys.

CHARLIE. Disc jockeys! Disc jockeys!

HARRY. Ashamed to have Harry meet your daughter? Well I'm telling you something: this is *my* shop; it's *my* life. If you're afraid of—of—of Cassy's accusing finger . . . (*He paces* c) By God! You've more gall . . . ! If the Twelve Disciples were reincarnated, you'd arrange them in a pop group.

CHARLIE (*hurt*) You're very frail tonight, mate.

HARRY. My mother's never said a harsh word about you. With all her pain and infirmity. "How's Charlie", she says.

CHARLIE. Why're you shoving your mother down my throat?

HARRY. She wouldn't "How's Charlie" if she knew you wanted to wrap her arthritis in a bloody block and tackle! (*He moves* R *to his basin, snatching up scissors and combs, throwing them down again, then round his chair to the shelves up* C) D'you know, I hope the police clutch on you, dear! Teach you a lesson. Twisted bitch! By God, ashamed of his daughter meeting *me*.

CHARLIE (*in almost a whisper*) Nothing personal.

(HARRY *moves down* L *and plugs in the kettle again*)

HARRY. Oogh, you're all intertwined, Charlie. (*Moving* c) One great big tube of non-sequitur.

(HARRY'S *turn of spirit gives us a first suspicion that Charlie is not always top dog.* CHARLIE *is subdued for a while. He "walks" his fingers along the bench*)

CHARLIE. I'd meet her at the station, Harry, but um—we haven't a clue what each other looks like.

HARRY. Wear your duffle coat, dear! Carry a copy of *Boys' Own* under your arm.

CHARLIE. Ha, yes. No—um, I'd rather—you know—meet her in private, really. By myself. Here.

HARRY. Should've thought of that before, as Nanny used to say.

CHARLIE. Thought've what?

HARRY (*shrugging*) *You* got married; *you* had the daughter. Well, now you've got *me*!

CHARLIE (*rising*) Yeah; don't I know it. (*He moves disconsolately to the window*)

HARRY. Yes—me! Dirty Harry Leeds, who fed you; taught you a trade when you flopped in the theatre.

CHARLIE. I beg yours! I beg yours! Couple more commercials, I'd be on top again.

HARRY. Pull the other, dear!

CHARLIE. Archy Selder only has a Series lined up for me, that's all! Just my own Series, dear!

HARRY. Really! You'll be turning in your clippers, then.

CHARLIE. What! I should rub a dub!

HARRY. Moving into the Hilton.

CHARLIE. Penthouse, mate. Penthouse!

HARRY (*moving to the front door up* C) Good! I'll clear out your side of the wardrobe.

CHARLIE (*moving up* C *to Harry*) You what! Can't wait till the body's cold? Can't wait till the body's cold?

HARRY. Well, we mustn't hold you back, Charlie! I'll chuck your stuff down.

CHARLIE. It's the middle of Sunday night, you twit.

HARRY. That's right.

CHARLIE. Where would I go?

HARRY. Straight into the Hilton, Charlie. You can interview Cassy in your Hartnell Suite.

CHARLIE. Oh the hell with Cassy! What're we bitching about?

HARRY. Because I'm too sordid for you.

CHARLIE. Oh shut the door, and calm down. Kettle's boiling. (*He picks up his cup from the bench*)

(HARRY *closes the door and moves down* L. *He pours water into the teapot*)

HARRY. I'd've given my back teeth to be married.

CHARLIE (*holding out his cup*) Who'd want your dirty old back teeth!

HARRY (*filling Charlie's cup with milk and tea*) It's caused me more embarrassment: the filthy questions they asked . . .

CHARLIE. Who asked?

HARRY. "Are you clean, Mr Leeds?"—"D'you live with your mother?"—"Who was that young man I saw you with last night?"

Charlie. Who's this? Who's this? Eh? Eh?

Harry (*pouring his own tea*) The mothers—parents—when I had that Scout Troop.

Charlie. Oh.

Harry. And my face flamed up; always blushed. I could see it coming: they'd stop me in the street. A bit of yack-yack, then slam below the belt: "Are you married?" And they had that raised-eyebrow'd purposeful disinterest. "No, I fear not"—"Oh-oh-oh-oh, aren't you! Mm, well little Johnny tells us *everything that happens*, Mr Leeds. And my face like the backside of a gibbon.

Charlie. Oh well. Never mind. (*He picks up his marzipan roll and sits in his chair*)

Harry. How dare they! How damn dare they!

Charlie. You're not tying yourself in knots, for God's sake? It's twenty years ago.

Harry (*going to sit in his chair*) It leaves a scar.

Charlie. Yes; well I shouldn't've trusted you, either. There never was such a short-trousered nobble-knee'd piker. Shouldn't've trusted you with me stuffed otter.

Harry. You never saw me in my scouting days.

Charlie. Never saw you! Never saw you! That first trip—very first trip—Hampton Court—your mother made us brawn butties.

Harry. I had my new suède jacket . . .

Charlie. You had your full khaki, dear. The lot. Long socks, dagger *and* a pole, no less. Talk about embarrassed!

(Harry *giggles shyly*)

Harry. Mm, I've always had a guilty conscience. Can't think why I went in uniform.

Charlie. Oh, you admit it *now*.

Harry. We-ell. I didn't know you then. Suppose I felt important; manly. Putting on a bit of style, I suppose.

Charlie. And as for the Maids of Honour Shop! You! Ordering a cream tea in French.

Harry (*giggling*) Yes. That was another time I blushed—

Charlie. —ducked under the table—

Harry. —pretended I'd dropped a spoon.

Charlie. Yes: you were gone ten minutes. Thought you'd had a come-over.

Harry. My blushes lasted longer than Worcester sauce in a church cupboard.

Charlie. Oh, get Rudyard Kipling! What! Witty, dear.

Harry. Long time since I last blushed, Charlie.

Charlie. I don't know why—with that lot wound on your head. (*He nods at Harry's bandages*)

Harry. Oh, don't start on that, Charlie. Please!

Charlie. You're a silly old twit, aren't you! (*Fondly*) By hell you are. (*He munches his marzipan roll*)

(HARRY *sips his tea: then, right out of the blue—*)

HARRY. I once went in a brothel.

CHARLIE. Right in the middle of me Battenburg!

HARRY. It shows I've been around.

CHARLIE. Go in khaki shorts, did you?

HARRY. No.

CHARLIE. Dagger and pole? Get a new badge for that, don't you?

HARRY. Give over, will you!

CHARLIE. Don't say you weren't issued with your Brothel Badge, mate! It's worn on the left arm between the one for getting knotted and the one for rubbing sticks together. Lovely! Sort of field of azure with a pair of discarded knickers on a tent pole.

HARRY (*angrily*) Oh belt up with your sneering, you sardonic runt!

CHARLIE. Thank you, Hilaire Belloc! We do turn nasty! Nice kick-up-the-hooter for someone who's merely trying to keep life cheery.

HARRY. Oogh, you're so deep! D'you think I don't realize how vicious you are underneath? All your cod jocularity with its slimy undertow. Needling, digging, cutting. Oh go to hell! (*after a pause*) I was telling you something interesting . . .

CHARLIE. I've heard it. Ten times I've heard your brothel tale.

HARRY. Damn liar.

CHARLIE. There was a man weeping on the staircase. Right?

HARRY. That's only part of it.

CHARLIE. Then a door flung open.

HARRY. Curtain. It was a curtain.

CHARLIE. And a woman with a cigarette burning her lips asked you to dance naked while she threw marmalade at your navel. I've heard it, mate. Heard it. You've nothing left I haven't seen and heard a thousand times—and you always end it the same way.

HARRY. End what?

CHARLIE. Your brothel tale. You pause; suck in your breath; and say, "How's that for Holy Week?" (*He flings his marzipan roll in his basin*) And if I once more hear you pause, suck in your breath, and say "How's that for Holy Week?", I'll stuff a skewer in me ear and go to hell as a kebab!

(*There is a pause*)

HARRY. I never know where I am with you, Charlie. One minute to the next; never know where I am.

CHARLIE. Spice of life.

HARRY. Have you ever thought about my name, Charlie: Harry Leeds? Harry C. Leeds. How d'you spell it?

CHARLIE. Going off your rocker?

HARRY. How d'you know I'm here? What proof have you that I exist? How d'you know I'm not imaginary?

(The door bell rings. CHARLIE *and* HARRY *rise. They stand in silence. After a while it rings again)*

HARRY. They wouldn't come on a Sunday. It's Sunday.

CHARLIE *(his voice trembling) Might* be Ronnie Unsworth.

HARRY. You'll have to go.

(The door bell rings)

They'll only keep on and on.

CHARLIE. You go. Peep through the keyhole.

(Both of them move to the door up C. CHARLIE *opens it, and* HARRY *moves into the lobby. After a while he returns)*

Man, is it?

HARRY. Yes.

CHARLIE. Policeman?

HARRY. Can't tell. He's standing in front of the keyhole.

CHARLIE. Oh, come out! *(He pulls Harry aside, to* R *of the door, then goes out into the lobby. After a second he returns, holding both hands over his mouth)*

HARRY. Is it?

CHARLIE *(nodding)* Policeman. Saw him through the keyhole.

HARRY. What's he doing?

CHARLIE. Nodding and smiling.

HARRY. Who at?

CHARLIE. *Me,* you fool! *(He closes the door)* He's crouched on the other side.

HARRY. What now?

CHARLIE. Bluff it out. Switch out the lights.

HARRY. Wait! He's opening the door!

(A tall shadow can be seen through the glass of the door. Soon there is a knock)

CHARLIE. God help us all and Oscar Wilde.

VOICE *(off)* Anyone there!

CHARLIE *(calling)* We're closed! Come tomorrow! *(He pushes Harry downstage)*

*(*CHARLIE *and* HARRY *whisper together)*

VOICE *(off)* Will you open up, please.

*(*CHARLIE *creeps back. Tentatively he opens the door a few inches)*

Mr Charles Dyer at home, sir?

CHARLIE. Possibly. Possibly. Why?

VOICE *(off)* Would *you* be Mr Charles Dyer?

CHARLIE. I'm a ratepayer, Officer. I mean, how do I know um, um. I've a right to see your identity card.

VOICE *(off)* Certainly, sir. Although it's quite unnecessary.

(A uniformed arm is seen—holding a card. CHARLIE *looks at it; the hand is withdrawn, and* CHARLIE *closes the door)*

CHARLIE (*whispering*) He's got a card.
HARRY. What's it say?
CHARLIE (*hopelessly*) Didn't like to look.
HARRY. Oh, you're rotten weak, you are.

(*There is another knock on the glass.* CHARLIE *slowly opens the door*)

VOICE (*off*) *Are* you Mr Dyer, sir?

(CHARLIE *nods glumly*)

CHARLIE (*whispering*) Yes.
VOICE (*off*) Ah. There we are then, sir. Good night.

(*The* POLICEMAN *hands Charlie a long buff envelope, then clumps away. The outside door bangs*) (CHARLIE *closes the shop door and wanders down* L)

HARRY (*following him*) I'd never've believed they'd deliver it on Sunday. (*He pats Charlie's shoulders*) It'll all work out.
CHARLIE (*in a tiny voice*) Yes.
HARRY. Um, what's it say?

(CHARLIE, *his fingers trembling, opens the envelope. He takes out an official paper and tries to read it; then he gives it to Harry*)

CHARLIE. You read it, Harry.
HARRY. Oh um, are you sure you want me to?
CHARLIE. It's a blur, Harry—all a blur, like seeing it in triplicate. Here . . . ! (*He hands over the document*)

(HARRY *begins reading it aloud, moving* C *and fumbling for his spectacles*)

HARRY. Um—"Information has been laid this day by Rychard Lees, Chief Constable . . ."
CHARLIE (*moving below his chair*) Yes, yes. Skip to the meat.
HARRY (*reading*) Um . . . Oh God! Listen, Charlie: ". . . that you did at the County Borough aforesaid at an establishment known as The Adam's Apple behave in a manner likely to cause a serious breach of the peace and did parade in female attire . . ." Oh God, Charlie!
CHARLIE. Read it, Harry! Read it!
HARRY (*reading*) ". . . and did importune in a manner calculated to bring—depravity . . ."

(CHARLIE *sinks into his chair.* HARRY *is himself near to tears*)

Oh hell, Charlie. (*Whispering*) Oh hell.
CHARLIE. Woosh—they've—they've really come thundering into Jordan, haven't they! I should rub-a . . . woosh! (*He looks old, tired, frightened*)
HARRY. Oh Charlie!
CHARLIE. When does it say?
HARRY (*reading*) "You are therefore summoned to appear before the Magistrates' Court sitting at the . . ."

Charlie. The date, dear! Date! I don't care if they're sitting on their potties. Get to the date!
Harry (*reading*) Yes. Um—blah blah blah—twenty-third of this month.

(Charlie *and* Harry *both count silently*)

Charlie. Ten days' time.
Harry. Nine. No, ten. Yes.
Charlie. 'F'only I could go now—tonight; get it done. Fourteen days torture already, Harry; and now another ten. Harry, read it again . . .

(*In a sudden vicious movement*, Harry *tears the summons and flings it down*)

Harry (*moving* rc) Goddam you, Charlie!

(Charlie *rises and kneels to retrieve the torn pieces*)

Charlie. What're you—what're you . . . !
Harry. Never told me all this, did you! "A mistake", it was—"victimization"—everyone shopping poor innocent Charlie.
Charlie. You trying to scuttle me? (*He moans over the torn papers*) There'll be a law against this.
Harry. Putting on drag—you forgot that bit!
Charlie. Drag! Drag?
Harry. Parading in female att— . . .
Charlie. It was me cabaret act, dear. Me old panto act. I borrowed the cigarette-girl's jumper; gave her a quid; pinched a hat and rolled up me trousers. (*He rises*) There's your drag, mate, I swear it. Oh, and I wrapped a tartan rug round for a skirt. Call that "drag"? Tell me! Honest!
Harry (*moving* c) And *after* you sat on Ed Chryslar's knee?
Charlie. You what! Oh, I should rub a dub: he's only married with five kids, dear!

(Harry *snatches the paper from Charlie's hand*)

Harry (*wearily*) I'll mend it. (*During the following dialogue, he searches the drawers and shelves up* c, *looking for sticky tape*)
Charlie (*sitting in his chair*) There's nothing wrong with Ed Chryslar, Harry. Nothing. Five kids. Five! He may have another by now.
Harry. *Yours*, Charlie?
Charlie (*between his teeth*) Cut that out! I'm telling you—Ed Chryslar married that sexy bit on the whatcher-me-call-it Show. Lovely girl. And he bet me five pounds I wouldn't do me impersonation of Lady Muck launching a battleship. (*Falsetto*) And All Who Sail In Her—you know that old thing I do. A gag, Harry. A straight-up gag, dear; and this stupid young copper—only a boy, Harry.

Only a boy, he was . . . (*Pointing to the shelves down* L) There's the sticky tape.

HARRY (*moving* L) Oh yes. (*He cuts the tape and pieces the document together*)

CHARLIE. It was so quick, you see. So quick. Policemen by the cartload: up the plugholes, under the skirting. Someone complained, you see. Rowdyism. That delicatessen next door. Ugly yob! Strike me dead if I even *sniff* another gherkin! There was nothing happening, you see; that was the trouble. We-e-ll, they daren't send coppers for nothing; wasting official petrol; so they stamped on Charlie! Oh yes. What! Run him in, dear—he's better than nothing. (*He shivers and rubs his arms*) Someone walked over me grave. (*He tries to laugh*) In fact, they're marking time.

(HARRY *gives him the mended summons*)

Oh, that's lovely, Harry. Nicely done. Ta. Ta.

(HARRY *nods, replaces the tape, and sits downstage on the bench*)

Whew! (*He rises, trying to subdue another fit of shivering*) You believe me, don't you, Harry? Y-y-you do believe me?

HARRY (*nodding*) Yes, but—but why did they take your name?

CHARLIE (*moving* C, *then standing above his chair*) It was this young copper, Harry. You see—I was on Ed Chryslar's knee and I pushed me t-t-tongue out and said, "Yarboo, arrest me!"—or something. You know what? *He bloody did!* This young copper. Kept pushing me; p-pushing me, Harry. People watching. Wretched, Harry—it w-was wretched. "Aw, come off!" I said. I said: "I'm old enough to be your father; your daddy," I said. "*Please*, I said. "Please, son . . . !" (*He drops his voice to a whisper. There are tears in his eyes*) They were going to put me in the Black M-Maria, Harry. If it hadn't been for the Inspector—nice elderly man—he checked me driving licence; sent me home. (*He wipes his eyes; blows his nose; then he forces himself into the attack*) But, by God, I'll prove 'em wrong! What! "May it please your Honour! I am an established member of the theatrical profession. Yes! *Profession, sir! And* a married man. Yes sir! *Married!*"

HARRY. Long time ago.

CHARLIE. I was married, mate. That's me. Nothing puffy with me, mate. *I'm normal. I* was married *with a baby*.

HARRY. Whom you haven't seen in twenty years. She's coming tomorrow, isn't she!

CHARLIE. Angel of doom! Are you *trying* to hang me? Trying to hang me, are you? Why don't you help me; give me some confidence? Because I *am* innocent, Harry. I *was* doing my old panto stuff. "Ladies and Gentlemen of the Jury . . ." Hear me through on this, Harry; pick holes; say what you like. I'll keep practising until the day. Oh, I'll prove 'em wrong. I'll prove 'em . . . "Ladies and Gentlemen of the Jury. Your Honour. I am an established member of the Theatrical Profession in good standing."—God, it's lucky I kept up me Equity! Right up to date—"Your Honour, my whole act is based upon the uproarious antics of my female impersonations. Top line. Top line female impersa—um—Was Dan Leno a puff? Was Henry Ainley? The great W. S. Pennington. Charlie's Aunt; all these wonderful names? No, sir. No, sir, old lad! Only five years since I made my farewell debut; they cheered. They stood and cried out: "Encore, Charlie!"—um, fifteen years, maybe . . . (*He stops; plucks his lip*) Harry, when did I do that Broker's Man at Streatham?

HARRY. Before the War?

CHARLIE. Oh God! Oh hell! (*He covers his mouth with his hand. He speaks in a tiny, quiet voice*) "Ladies and Gentlemen of the Jury, I'm a small-time back-street hairdresser; and I don't know why I—just a gag; bit of fun! Please give me a break."

(HARRY *rises and moves* LC)

HARRY. You've done all those little film bits; and that commercial.

CHARLIE (*shrugging him off and moving away* C) *I* know. *I* know. Which—um—which commercial?

HARRY. The duffle coat one. Everyone'd know that.

CHARLIE. Yes, but um—I needed one where I was—well, where I was dressed as a woman—to prove my case. But it's getting on for thirty years, Harry. I can hardly say I was rehearsing, can I? By hell, this'll ruin me Come-Back.

(HARRY *sits in Charlie's chair* LC)

HARRY. Don't fret, Charlie. It'll be all right.

CHARLIE (*spiritedly*) You needn't bolster me, dear. I'm not bothered. I'll handle my own case, that's why. What'm I in the theatre for? Eh? I'll tell 'em! I'll show I'm an old pro. God, if I can't use my personality to—to . . . (*He shakes his head*) Oh Christ, Harry, I'm so f-frightened. (*He flops at Harry's feet*)

(HARRY *cradles Charlie in his lap, stroking his head and rocking him backwards and forwards*)

HARRY. Don't fret, Charlie. Don't fret. We'll see. We'll—see, Charlie.

CHARLIE. I'm innocent, Harry. Innocent.

HARRY. Oh Charlie—you poor old bugger

CHARLIE. Yes. (*He sits back on his haunches. He tries to smile*) D'you ever see two such frail old twits!

HARRY. But you won't be alone, Charlie; at the trial. I'll come with you.

CHARLIE. You! Come with me? God no, they'd give me ninety years.

CURTAIN

Scene 2

Scene—*The same. Half an hour later.*

When the Curtain *rises,* Charlie *is discovered slumped in his chair, a shawl round his shoulders, thoroughly woe-begone. Every now and then he gives a sob; his eyes are red. The front door bangs (off). Then* Harry *enters. He wears a macintosh which is dripping, and a sou-wester over his bandages. For a while he stands up* C, *stamping his feet and blowing water from his face; brushing the rain from his raincoat. Then he moves down* C *and hands Charlie a packet of aspirins.*

Harry. Had to go all the way to that machine on the corner.

Charlie. You'd've got 'em at the pub, stupid twit.

Harry (*hedging*) Could I?

Charlie. Where's the gin? You haven't forgotten the gin?

Harry. They were closed, you see. Pub was closed.

Charlie. Not the back door.

Harry. I didn't like. I'm—I'm no good at back doors, Charlie. You go for some.

Charlie. Oh yes! God lighting fires under me sinuses—I feel like traipsing through floods for gin! I should rub a dub. (*He chews two aspirins, grimacing*) Better make some of your lousy char to wash 'em down.

Harry. Surely. (*He hangs his damp clothes in the stock room*)

Charlie. There's a smell of gas in there. Reckon that jet's blown out again.

Harry. No, it hasn't.

Charlie. Smells like it. Just the right size for a tomb, that stock room.

Harry (*moving* R *of Charlie*) Might be handy at a pinch.

Charlie. That kind of talk's against God, Harry. Oh yes, dear. Hallelujah or no hallelujah, let's keep the jet going. I should rub a dub.

Harry. Your eyes aren't half red.

Charlie. Only the white parts.

(Charlie *turns away, but* Harry *leans forward to see*)

Keep to yourself! You look like a pregnant hen. Have you seen your hips? Have you? Ever seen 'em? Far too wide for a man. Oh yes. A real man has great broad withers which taper to powerful flanks: what one might call the crutch of the matter. And look at you! Hen is too delicate a term. Um, pelican! Yes! You're a pregnant pelican, mate. (*He has another look at Harry. He points to Harry's bandages*) Bit much when you even pad sou'westers with 'em!

Harry. I feel safer. Have you worked anything out?

Charlie. Have I hell! I'm right in it, dear. No escape: I've as much chance of shoving straw in the pouch of a thirst-maddened wallaby. Anyway, sufficient unto the day, mate. I should care.

(Harry *moves above Charlie and looks in the tea tin down* l)

I'm innocent. Oh, belt up reminding me!

Harry. Oh—we've used all the tea; unless Mum has a spot in her cupboard.

Charlie. No! Don't! Let's leave—sleeping things up there.

(Harry *takes a bar of chocolate from the shelf*)

Harry. Here! How about some drinking chocolate?

Charlie. Yes.

(Harry *scutters childishly in the corner down* l, *plugging in the kettle and unwrapping his bar of chocolate*)

(*Out of the blue*) You needn't start increasing the rent, Harry.

Harry. Whose rent? Mother doesn't charge you rent.

Charlie. *You*, mate! *You* needn't increase the rent.

Harry (*tetchily*) I'm not with you, Charlie. Spell it for me: 's'too early in the morning for obscurity.

Charlie. I mean don't slop and slap in the pity of it all; don't talk nice and *be* nice; and above all, dear—above all, don't expect anything for it—no tail wagging.

(Harry *starts shredding chocolate into a cup*)

Because—(*his voice trembles, but he pulls himself together*)—because I'll be giving you nothing, mate. (*He rises and stretches largely*) Aye-yi-yi-yi-yi! Soon be dawn, I reckon. (*He moves to Harry*) What're you up to?

(Harry *does not answer*)

Eh? What's all this?

Harry. If you had a teeniest scrap of thought for anyone; if you had . . .

Charlie. Very well, I'm sorry. I'm sorry. I'm sorry. But no preaching, please! What're you messing at?

Harry (*after a deep sigh*) I'm shredding this chocolate bar, like—like me and my sisters used to do. Long after midnight—sneaking downstairs for hot water—all of us giggling. And my auntie, too; she was with us; she's alive still. She only has six skins. You're supposed to have seven; but auntie's only got six.

Charlie. She rides low in the saddle.

Harry. Oh, you silly bitch! (*He giggles*)

(Charlie *smiles slightly*)

Charlie. God help us all and Oscar Wilde. I'm living with a schoolgirl. (*At Harry*) Are we going to suck-suck scrumchy choccy, are we?

(HARRY *pours hot water into his concoction.* CHARLIE *watches and shudders*)

Urrgh, it looks vile! Like some ghastly brew for the Circumcision Rites of the dreaded Mumba Wumbas.

(HARRY *licks his lips uneasily.* CHARLIE *pushes home his advantage*)

D'you like cooking, dear? Do you, love? Catch me drinking *that*! I tell you, Harry, you're a dizzy Lizzy. All soft. Your hands're soft; your shoulders are soft; and your hips are too wide for a man.

HARRY. And you repeat yourself. You say everything twice.

CHARLIE. Who does? Who does?

HARRY. There you are! A double "who does".

CHARLIE. We-ell.

HARRY. Think your every word is so divine, everyone—including God, is panting for a duplicate.

CHARLIE (*haughtily*) Really, Well, for your information, tit-face, *you* just said "every" twice; *and* you've an exasperating twitch at mealtimes.

HARRY. Little mannerisms . . .

CHARLIE. Mannerisms! Mannerisms! I've had twenty years of that hole in your face and no sooner do you put a fork near it than you sniff and jerk your head to the left (*He demonstrates*) Like that! I'll do it again. Up comes the fork . . . (*He does it two or three times*) Sniff; jerk; stuff! Sniff; jerk; stuff! An outright twitch, dear. What! Touch of the palsy, mate! That's you. Probably degenerate into a sniffing, jerking, stuffing jelly. (*Moving below his chair*) Want to watch it, dear; bits and pieces'll begin dropping off because of the vibration. (*He sits and swings round in his chair, laughing*)

HARRY. At least, I don't cut my toe-nails in the kitchen.

CHARLIE. Once! Once in all my life.

HARRY. It was enough.

CHARLIE. And who never empties the teapot?

HARRY (*moving* L *of Charlie's chair*) And who leaves the basin filthy and never washes her razor?

CHARLIE (*yelling*) She hasn't time! After you've hogged the closet for hours, puffing yourself up! So help me—if ever I reach heaven, there'll be two toilets!

HARRY. And if I reach heaven, someone else'll be cleaning them.

CHARLIE. Heaven! *You!* Ha! On second thoughts, yes: I can just visualize you—a bleached poppy in a coterie of deceased giggling gentlemen; illuminated wolf cubs saluting in a pink mist of cherubimic bottoms and sugar lumps. And by Hell, Harry, if I'm Up There—I'll jump slap in the middle of you all—*and belch*! (*He swings round and round in his chair, rubbing his hands in evil anticipation*)

HARRY (*dryly*) We shan't be taken aback—having heard rumours of your arrival.

(CHARLIE *swings his chair to a stop and surveys Harry*)

CHARLIE. Mmm. On our smug stint, are we? Our slightly-gloating stint?

HARRY. More your line, Charlie.

CHARLIE. You're an insidious creep, aren't you! Enigma—enigma's the word; sometimes a willowy thing giggling at big words and sometimes a clutching goblin with a goat on your navel. You've got me. I see it now.

HARRY. Oh. It's all my fault, is it?

CHARLIE. You're dead right, it is. Dead right! Twenty years you've had me. There I am—doing fine. Empress. Third on the Bill! You pick me up in a Maids of Honour shop; and you *did* pick me up, Harry—with your dagger and scout pole.

HARRY (*pityingly*) Oh no, Charlie. No.

CHARLIE. *You picked me up!* And matriculated me to the glory of a two-bit back-street barber.

HARRY. I came down to see if I could help. (*Moving towards the door*) I'm not staying.

CHARLIE. You came down to gloat, mate! To rub your hands, to lick your lips; to taste the shame and excitement, without any of the danger. Oooogh, he's going to Court; he's going to Court; Charlie's going to Court! "I'll come with you, Charlie," he said! "You won't be alone!" *I'll be the loneliest old bugger on earth!* (*He pushes his fist to his mouth and pauses to control himself*) You'll be there—my daughter'll be there—the old sow'll be there—and I'll be the lonelist ex-Third-on-the-Bill. What! I should rub a dub. (*He thumps the arm of his chair*) And I'm *innocent*, I'm *innocent*!

HARRY (*moving down* c *towards him*) Charlie . . .

CHARLIE. Get off! Get away! Get back to your stinking pit, dear. The show's over. Midnight matinee. Over. Finished.

(HARRY *moves to the door*)

(*Yelling after him*) And all God's children have toe-nails! All of 'em! It's a kind of thin horn, provided by the Almighty, for the protection of our digits. There is nothing rude or disgusting. Queen Victoria had 'em; you have 'em; and all the ladies in your Presbyterian Church Choir have 'em—except that bitch who sings the solos; and she has hooves.

(HARRY *moves down to him*)

HARRY. All this is vengeance, pure and simple. You won't be told; you won't be helped; you're never wrong, and if you're in a hole you drag everyone down with you.

CHARLIE. This is *you* we're describing, mate!

HARRY. *You* started it with the teapot.

CHARLIE. I beg yours. I beg yours! You said I repeated myself.

HARRY. You said I twitched.

CHARLIE. Toe-nails! Toe-nails!

HARRY. And I say it again. As long as I'm cooking and scrubbing—

CHARLIE. Great! Here comes the hot-washing-machine stint!

HARRY. —as long as I'm cooking and scrubbing for you, Charlie, you can keep your filthy nail clippings out of my kitchen. Period! (*He moves to the door*) I'll bet Victoria never cut her nails in the kitchen.

(HARRY *exits up* C, *slamming the door.* CHARLIE *rises, hurries to the door, opens it, and yells upstairs*)

CHARLIE. No—she did 'em in the Music Gallery! (*He slams the door, then opens it again and shouts*) Harry! *Harry!!*

(HARRY *returns*)

HARRY. Sssh! What?

CHARLIE (*indicating the shop*) It's—so quiet; so much room for thoughts. I um, don't mind risking my life with some of that—black brew. (*He sits in his chair*)

HARRY (*moving down* L) Don't do me any favours, dear.

(*A silence follows.* HARRY *potters. He mixes hot water with his concoction—to freshen it, then he pours two mugsful, and brings one to Charlie*)

CHARLIE. No sugar?

(HARRY *sighs. He returns to the table with the mugs, puts sugar in each, then comes back to Charlie.* CHARLIE *grabs his drink.* HARRY *goes and sits in his chair with his own mug. They both take some while before actually sipping, and afterwards,* HARRY's *face lights with pleasure. The drink is a success! But* CHARLIE *merely grunts; and after a few sips, he nods at Harry's bandages*)

When're they coming off, then?

HARRY. I will take them off, Charlie. I—er . . .

CHARLIE. When? When?

HARRY (*shaking his head*) A—a bit longer. Charlie. I feel safe with these, you see. Be awful without them now—empty—unclean.

(CHARLIE *sighs deeply. He looks around the shop*)

CHARLIE. We had such wonderful plans, didn't we!

HARRY. Yes.

CHARLIE. Wonderful plans, we had.

HARRY (*nodding*) Hydraulic chairs; shell-shaped basins—

CHARLIE. —wrought iron on the bloody striped pole—

HARRY. —tinted mirrors; and that boy with the hairy arms'd've painted us murals.

CHARLIE. Could have expanded upstairs: salon de dames. Tea and crumpet under the driers.

HARRY. Parfums; boutiques.

CHARLIE. Branches in Bond Street—

HARRY. —Muswell Hill—

CHARLIE. Muswell Hill!! Are you mad?

HARRY. 'S'part of the set-up. All the nobs have suburban branches. Make a packet, dear.

CHARLIE. Right. Muswell Hill.

HARRY. Paris. Brussels.

CHARLIE. Amsterdam. New York!

HARRY. And then me hair falls out! Bluddyell!

(HARRY *sits groaning, but* CHARLIE—*lips licked wickedly, eyes gleaming with evil relish—begins to recount—*)

CHARLIE. I was telling your mother: "Overnight, Mrs Leeds", I said. "There it was," I said, "on his pillow." Oh, the shock! "Harry," I shouted. "Your hair, mate! Look at your suffering hair. On the pillow!" I should rub a dub. You went white. Did you know you went white and started screaming?

HARRY (*nodding*) Like finding me own eyeball. That's the only way I could describe it to someone like you, Charlie, who still has hair. Think how you'd feel, finding your eye looking at you and one side of your face all black.

CHARLIE. Urrgh. You always were a messy talker. No breeding; no culture.

HARRY. I was trying to make you appreciate . . .

CHARLIE. I don't have to appreciate empty eye sockets, mate. It was me wakened you, wasn't it?

HARRY (*nodding*) Horrible.

CHARLIE. Thought it was a kitten curled on your pillow. "Where did he get a kitten?" I thought. I was going to stroke it. Stroke it, dear! (*He puts out his hand and draws it back*) Oh my God! Well, you always did have a funny head, Harry. I mean, you did, dear; but all hairless! Like a washerwoman's elbow, it was.

HARRY. Can't you shut up! Call yourself a friend—knowing how I suffer?

CHARLIE (*casting his glance at the ceiling and muttering*) Now for the great martyr stint.

HARRY. Ever since my first little bare patch it's been the same. It was you who first told me. D'you remember? "Oogh, you're going bald," you said. "D'you know?" Of course I bloody knew. I wanted to forget, not be reminded. (*He rises, takes his mug to the basin* R *and washes it*) People don't realize it's an affliction like anything else.

CHARLIE. Really? Cause you great pain, does it? Great pain—falling hair?

HARRY (*moving* C) The pain's in here and up here! (*He taps his heart and head*) A little understanding, that's all, Charlie. You don't rush up to a limping man and say: "Hey, you've only one leg, did you know?" You're all polite; you make excuses: "Really? I never knew you had tin legs, wall eyes and a goitre." But see a bald man and it's everybody's tee-hee time. "Your head's coming through your hair, mate!" "Hello, Curly!" "Hey, want your bonce polished for two-pence?" Being bald's an affliction. A human problematic affliction.

CHARLIE. Too blasted true! It's afflicting you, afflicting me, the business, everything.

HARRY. Wish we'd made it a car accident now; or a bandit with a cosh. You talked me into a falling beam.

CHARLIE. All our customers appreciate this is old property. Nothing more natural than a bit of woodworm in the cellar. Not that you can live for ever swathed in swaddling.

HARRY. 'S' only seven weeks.

CHARLIE. *Only!* D'you know what Ronnie Unsworth said yesterday? "Is it my imagination," he said, "or are Harry's bandages getting bigger?"

HARRY. He didn't, did he?

CHARLIE. Harry, they *are* getting bigger! Each fresh morning sees another layer. Talk about woodworm—more like you've been trampled by bison. And you've a beautiful wig in there you refuse to wear. (*He nods at the stock room*) A beautiful wig.

HARRY. It doesn't work, Charlie. (*Moving down* L *with the mug*) I've tried it. (*He puts the mug on the shelf*)

CHARLIE. You're worse than Fanny with her first bottom set!

HARRY (*moving above Charlie's chair to* C) I've nothing to join it to, d'you see? My neck's naked, Charlie.

CHARLIE (*putting his mug on the floor*) Bit of scribble round the edges with an eyebrow pencil. Perishing barber who can't sketch a tuft of hair. I'll do it for you myself. Now.

(CHARLIE *rises and lunges at* HARRY, *who backs off* R, *squealing and cuddling his arms over his head.* CHARLIE *follows*)

No disgrace, y'know—alopecia. Bishops get alopecia. A well-known *thing*—alopecia. Alopecia is . . .

HARRY (*yelling*) Will you shut up! Carping swine. (*Quietly*) I might try tomorrow. I'll remove the bandages and . . .

CHARLIE. God—you sound like the light that failed!

HARRY. I said I'd try—you carping swine!

CHARLIE. I've had twenty years of your moaning, mate; and for once I crave a bright breezy statement: "Off they come tomorrow, Charlie!" That's what I crave—not the dingy inference of an oncoming Amen.

HARRY (*shouting*) All right! Tomorrow. I'll unwrap tomorrow!

CHARLIE (*shouting*) Thank you, Mummy!

HARRY. But no jibes, Charlie—like Monday's Pimple.

CHARLIE. Monday's what?

HARRY. Last Monday, that heat lump on top of my head. You said I looked like Cleopatra's titty.

CHARLIE. Oh? (*Pause*) Oh yes.

HARRY. What're you laughing at?

CHARLIE. I wasn't. (*Pause*) Monday's Pimple! Thought you'd created a new Doctor Series. "Monday's Pimple" starring Sherry Clade and . . .

HARRY. Shut your face! I've begged you! No jibes.

CHARLIE (*moving to his chair and sitting; purposefully calm*) As you will, dear. As you will. Just discard the Maharajah stint; I'll be happy.

(*There is a pause*)

HARRY. I appreciate you're trying shock tactics, Charlie.

CHARLIE. It's nothing. Nothing. Doesn't matter.

HARRY (*moving* c) Yes it does. I must convince myself the World looks into my eyes; not at my skin. Damn it! I'll do it! I'll face them. I'll take up me comb, scissors and me clippers . . .

CHARLIE. You'll what! I beg yours, dear! You're not stepping into this shop, Harry. A bald hair stylist! You must be empty inside as well, thank you and hello the unemployed benefit.

HARRY. But where shall I go?

CHARLIE. Upstairs, dear. Up the kitchen flue. I don't care; but not in here with your wretched affliction.

HARRY (*moving above him to the window*) You're horrid! You're inhuman; monstrous.

CHARLIE. Oh yes. Lovely. And how am I supposed to offer a bottle of shampoo or a nice friction massage? "Bluddyell," they'll say, "is that what happened to *him*?"

HARRY (*crossing above Charlie to* c) The devil have you, Charlie Dyer! Rotten tormentor.

CHARLIE. Yes, I should rub a dub; here's us with a stock room of hair restorer—ten bob a go including the dropper; and you, Cleopatra's Titty, in the next chair. What! There's a nice ta-ta for a cold morning on the Left Bank!

HARRY (*sitting in his chair*) Oh God!

CHARLIE. Your clipping days are over, dear.

HARRY. I'll die.

CHARLIE (*rising and putting his mug on the basin* L) You and your one-legged men with wall eyes! (*Moving* c) Be polite as you wish, you never find 'em in the Royal Ballet, do you?

HARRY. I'll swallow the stock room gas. Sniff it till I'm gone.

CHARLIE (*moving* L *of Harry*) I'm asking if you find knock-knee'd men in the Royal Ballet?

HARRY (*shouting*) No. No. No. (*He rises and moves away* R)

CHARLIE. Then there you have it, dear, haven't you. There you have it. So what with me and me magistrates, and you and your alopecia, we'll have a right happy Tonsorium, shan't we!

(HARRY *bursts into tears and flings himself to the ground, sobbing bitterly.* CHARLIE *flops into his chair*)

I reckon I'll write a pantomime. (*He nods*) Write a pantomime and call it "Noddy in Hell".

CURTAIN

ACT II

SCENE—*The same. Some hours later.*

Outside, street lamps still shine but the sun is rising. A neon light is flashing somewhere. A lonely lorry lumbers up a distant hill.

When the CURTAIN *rises,* CHARLIE *is discovered sitting on the floor* C, *his back against his chair. He is wearing pyjamas, with a shawl around his shoulders. Steps sound on the stairs. The shop door opens.* HARRY *enters in his dressing gown and pyjamas, and carrying Charlie's dressing gown. He switches on the lights and moves, blinking and yawning, to Charlie* C. *He hands Charlie the dressing gown.*

HARRY. Why don't you come back to bed? You'll catch cold in your bones, sitting on the floor. You'll get piles.

CHARLIE. D'you know, Harry, you should write poetry for anniversary cards. You have such a silver flow of oratory. You could bring a new delicacy to contemporary literature: "Dearest Grandma, Full of Smiles. A Happy Birthday to your Piles!"

HARRY. It isn't half late. Long past dawn. Have you been weeping again?

CHARLIE. Oh belt up! What're you doing—working up an Agony Column? Feel like a fly in a milk bottle: can't breathe without *you* clucking round the brim. I'm in trouble so I'm the teensy-weeniest bit sad. It's natural, isn't it?

HARRY. Oh yes.

CHARLIE. Mental met-man! Checking if I'm damp or dry.

HARRY. Sorry.

CHARLIE. Oh, I'm worried a bit, that's all. It's not what you've done that counts—it's the way they describe it. And I'm petrified they'll—well, you know what they said about you when you had that scout troop.

HARRY. Oh well, they just used to ask if I was married, you see, Ch—— . . .

CHARLIE. Yes, yes, that's what I mean. And with me being artistic . . .! See the old Judge up there. They'll crucify me, Harry.

(HARRY *goes and sits in his chair*)

Everyone free from stain except Dirty Charlie. The way that copper'll paint me, I'll have asked him for a kiss in the bargain. And I'm innocent, Harry. As God's my witness, I did it for a gag.

HARRY. There's a new law—consenting males or something.

CHARLIE. Oh God help us all and Oscar Wilde! I was on Ed Chryslar's knee: he's as butch as Kong, dear. Been married to half Charing Cross Road. I need no laws. Need no laws.

HARRY. No. No, but I thought—you know—I mean—won't Ed Chryslar speak for you?

CHARLIE. They hate getting mixed, you see. Oh yes, I've um—rung three times; and heard a click! He's living with Sherry Clade. Lovely girl. I was in a show with her.

HARRY. Go to their house.

CHARLIE. Mm, I'll see Archy Selder before the day. Archy'll give me some help. He's my agent, Archy Selder.

HARRY. Has been for twenty years.

CHARLIE. Yes.

HARRY. Oh well, you've much to be thankful for.

CHARLIE. Oh yes! What! If I fell head first in a bog you'd say me shoes were clean.

HARRY. I mean you've had a good life and . . .

CHARLIE. What're you doing—laying me out? Laying me out, are you?

HARRY. No: I'm admiring you for having lived to the full, that's all.

CHARLIE. Off me own bat, mate. Nobody's helped me.

HARRY. Possibly not. You know, you talk about goldfish bowls . . .

CHARLIE. Goldfish bowls? Goldfish bowls? Who talks about goldfish bowls? *I* don't talk about goldfish bowls.

HARRY. I hadn't finished, dear.

CHARLIE. Working up a new fetish, are you? New fetish?

HARRY (*rising and moving to the bench*) Oh suit yourself—going to be clever. (*He picks up a newspaper which has been folded at the crossword*)

CHARLIE. Wilting under me badinage, then? On the wilting stint?

HARRY (*vaguely sulking*) Nope. (*Muttering*) Horoscope. Horoscope . . . (*He wanders up* C)

CHARLIE. You what?

HARRY. It's a clue. (*He searches through the shelves up* C) Seen my dictionary, Charlie?

CHARLIE. That novelty thing from a cracker?

HARRY (*moving to the shelves down* L) It was Margie's—my sister's. (*He searches in the shelves and cupboards* L)

CHARLIE. Not surprised: it hasn't a single filthy word. I was checking yesterday.

(HARRY *moves an antique deed-box from the cupboard*)

Mind me box! (*He jumps up, flings the shawl on the bench, and takes the box from Harry*) Full of me mother's mementoes, this. (*Crossing* R) History! History, it is. (*He puts it on the stool*)

HARRY (*discovering his pocket dictionary at the back of the cupboard*) Ah! (*Then—*) There's a bottle at the back here. (*He produces a bottle of gin*)

CHARLIE (*hurrying* L) Bluddyell! (*He snatches the bottle*)

HARRY. It's the one Ronnie Unsworth sent for my birthday.
CHARLIE. Many happy returns! Get the glasses!
HARRY (*taking two tumblers from the shelf* L) You might well grab! It's more yours—the money you've spent on him.
CHARLIE. Belt up nagging! Disc jockey this; Harry Unsworth that! Give me a kiss, I'll tell you who's peculiar! Ho, ho, ha, ha!

(HARRY *holds the glasses and* CHARLIE *pours two tots of gin.* CHARLIE *then knocks his back*)

HARRY (*toasting*) All the best, Charlie, love. Hope everything works out well. (*He sees Charlie knocking back his gin, shrugs to himself and drinks. He then picks up his dictionary and sits in his own chair*)

(CHARLIE *puts on his dressing gown*)

Now—Horoscope. It'll say if it's Greek here—Horo—Hig—Hol—Hoopoe.
CHARLIE (*moving* C) Hoopoe! What in great thumping charity's Hoopoe?
HARRY (*reading*) Er—Hoopoe. South European bird with variegated plumage and large erectile crest.
CHARLIE. Filthy beast! (*He grabs the dictionary and throws it aside. Then he gives Harry the gin bottle and goes to the stool. He puts his glass on the basin, takes the box, and sits on the stool*) All me mother's little treasures in here. Look at this. (*He holds up a book, open, with a crushed flower within it*) A crushed rose in her Golden Treasury. A feathery crushed rose from Yesterday.
HARRY (*putting the newspaper beside his chair*) Always detested me—your mother.
CHARLIE (*brandishing the book*) Nineteen-O-Something-or-Other she filed a frail flower. (*He pops the rose back*) Twittering, giggling and pretty; look at her now! A ninety-year-old walnut. (*He rises, takes the glass and box to his own chair*) If her head was filleted, she'd look like a rusty prune. Oh, the sad, sad shrivelled bitch. There's but one blessing, mate! She's past worrying about hormones—male, female or variegated. I reckon that hoopoe's as queer as a coot, anyhow. (*He sits, with the box on his lap*)
HARRY. That's how the aborigines do them.
CHARLIE. Do who?
HARRY. Shrunken heads. They sort of fillet them and stuff hot pebbles through the earholes.
CHARLIE. Urrgh, you sadistic madam!
HARRY. Talented people, aborigines.
CHARLIE. Aborigines! We're discussing my mother. Do you mind! Twit! God, me mind boggles at how that veiny grizzled bag was once a twittering nymph from whose pure little womb I . . . (*His lips quiver*) Oh, Harry . . . !
HARRY. Yes, I only wish she understood me better.

CHARLIE. Too late now. Bones cracking; tissues rotten; mind gone. She didn't know me last time I went. Did I tell you?

HARRY (*rising to fill Charlie's glass; nodding*) Smelly thing—growing old. (*He sits again*)

CHARLIE. "Hello, dear," I said. "Hello," I said; but she just munched her gums; dribbling spit and a lump of puddin' on her chin. Lips all puckered and tuckered like a badly stitched haggis. (*He gulps gin and wipes his eyes on his sleeve*) Screwing me up, this gin is. (*He sniffs*) I'd been there half-an-hour; then all of a sudden: "Who are you?" she said. "*Who are you!*" What! "I'm your bloody son, dear," I said. "Silly old bitch," I said; but it didn't move her. Eyes all faded. Mental block, d'you see, Harry. (*He begins to weep*) She h-hates me so m-much . . .

HARRY (*rising to c, with the bottle and his glass*) It was her who made you, Charlie.

CHARLIE. Yes! Yes, mate! And I reckon God's punishing me, Harry.

HARRY (*ponderously*) Maybe He's punishing your mother.

(CHARLIE *pauses a second, impressed*)

CHARLIE. That was very deep, Harry. Very deep; and quite beautiful. And she's been expensive, Harry. Cost pounds a week, my mother has, you know. Pounds. It's been difficult. Difficult. I mean, if I'd had a few quid to myself, I might've got married again.

HARRY. Oh, be logical.

CHARLIE. What d'you mean—logical! How dare you! How bloody dare you! Many a woman I could've had. Many! I'm not like you—with your antennas and scout poles! Hundreds of women I could've had.

HARRY (*filling Charlie's glass*) Yes: well, you had your mother.

CHARLIE. Too true. Oh Harry—it's an awful place she's in. The Matron'd put the wind up Edgar Poe's ghost. I'm afraid to visit after dark. I really am. Stairs creakin' like groanin' monks; draughts shrieking up the chain mail. And you remember that vulture in the hall? Glass case? I'll swear it's not dead. Crossed pikes over the lavatory doors. I was in agony me last visit—I wouldn't "go", dear. Pull the chain in that place—drop in a snake pit!

HARRY (*putting the bottle on the basin* R, *then sitting in his chair*) Yes, you'd think they'd splosh a bit of sunny pink. I did my mother's room from top to bottom.

CHARLIE. Rubbing it in, are you? On the triumphant stint? (*Tenderly, he opens the poetry book*) My mother—who once pressed a rose.

> "So softly creeps the warming light
> And gently fades the loving night . . ."

Bastard! (*He rises, hurls the book down and stamps on it*) Blasted pressed rose! Pandora's blasted box! (*He puts the box on the table down* L) What am I going to tell her? I'll—I'll miss me visiting days! (*He *returns to his chair and sits*) What am I going to say? "Guess what, Mummy! They're calling me a puff!"

HARRY. It'll only be a fine, Charlie.

CHARLIE. You think so? You really think so?

HARRY. At very most.

CHARLIE. Yes. (*He nods*) Yes. (*And then—*) A *fine!* You've a blasted cheek: *I'm innocent.* Oh, God help us all and Oscar Wilde.

HARRY (*after a pause*) I sometimes wonder what they say—you know, Charlie—upstairs—when my sister calls on *my* mother.

CHARLIE. Ten whole days!

HARRY. I can just hear Margie yacking: "How old's Harry, now, Mum?" she'd say: and Mum'd say: "I don't know. How old is he?"

CHARLIE. Circular conversation.

HARRY. But that's how they talk.

CHARLIE. Should live in a turret!

HARRY. Yes; and Margie'd say: "He's old enough to've been married." Then she'd say—I can just hear her—"Mum, d'you think he's—he's a . . ." (*He bites his lip and grips the arms of his chair. He sits awhile, shaking his head*)

CHARLIE. What time're you due in Court? Eh? Eh? This is *my* wake, not yours, dear.

HARRY. I'd go to Court ten times to have your hair.

CHARLIE. And I'd swap every lock to stay out, mate. What! That's where God's so clever, you see.

HARRY. When I was over at Margie's last year . . .

CHARLIE. Oh, is she back again?

HARRY. No, listen: I had, well, a dreadful experience. I was bouncing their little boy on my knee. Gurgling; chubby. He's about three. And he threw his arms round my neck and pushed his peanut nose in my ear; and, oh Charlie, I couldn't help hugging and squeezing him. "Oh you darling darling thing," I whispered. Then it all happened.

CHARLIE. Happened? What happened?

HARRY. The baby—began screaming. Wouldn't stop. Then Dick ran in—all diddems and waddems. "What did you do?" he said. "What did you do?" His voice thick and accusing: face all over the front of his head. (*He sighs deeply*) How can you tell a man with hairs curling over his collar that you only wanted someone to hug; something to love?

CHARLIE. Kids! You get 'em on lease; get 'em on lease until they're fourteen; then they shove on tight trousers, and accuse you of stunting their growth!

HARRY. But to have a baby . . .

CHARLIE. You're maudlin. Your eyeballs're frothing with gin. I can hear 'em bubblin'.

HARRY. Ah but, Charlie: if you and me—you know, if we could've had a little lad of our own. All our own, to teach and cherish. Oh, I'd've loved him till he popped.

CHARLIE. Babies! The one reason we like 'em, they're the only living creatures more stupid than us.

HARRY. They wouldn't let us, anyhow. Such a shame; but they wouldn't give a baby to our kind.

CHARLIE (*rising and going down* L) Speak for yourself, mate! *I've had one.* (*He looks in his mother's box*) Hello! (*He finds something in the box*) Lock of hair! Good God, it's mine! A lock of me infant's hair! (*His lips quiver*) Oh-oh, H-Harry! Worms're crawling in me stomach and screaming for those dear dead days! (*He slams the box lid*) Bastard! Bastard! Hate me mother! Always did!

HARRY (*rising, picking up the bottle, and filling both glasses*) There, there. Have another gin. (*He puts the bottle on the floor and holds out Charlie's glass*)

CHARLIE. Oh my poor shrivelled Mammie—stuck in that resting place of elephants. Antique bucks and bitches, all death trumpets and grey sagging leather. One camp bed; one cane chair; and eight cubic feet for dying in. *I'm pulling her out!* Today! *Today!* Back she comes!

HARRY. Pulling her out where?

CHARLIE (*moving* C) Here. Home, where she belongs. (*He takes his tumbler*)

HARRY. In *my* home?

CHARLIE. She'll not bother you. Fit in upstairs.

HARRY. *My* mother's fitted up there.

CHARLIE. Yes. Lovely. Lovely. Muck in together. Lovely.

HARRY. Oogh, you're clever, you are, Charlie. Break me heart, fill me with gin; then creep your mother into me attic.

CHARLIE. Have another gin . . .

HARRY. You're not stuffin *my* house with sagging leather. (*He moves below his chair*)

CHARLIE. Well! This is it, then. What! The treacherous stint! Treacherous stint.

HARRY. Afraid to tell Matron why you won't be visiting Mummy for ninety days.

CHARLIE. Oh! Got me inside now! There's a nice monocle for a blind man, you bastard!

HARRY. The Matron was a very nice lady, *I* thought.

CHARLIE. Bats of a feather, dear! Bats of a feather!

HARRY. Now you listen, Charlie . . . (*He holds Charlie's arm*)

(CHARLIE *shakes him off*)

CHARLIE. No I won't. Get off! (*He moves round his chair to up* C)

HARRY. Never face me, will you! Rotten fungus-face! Never admit the truth . . .

CHARLIE (*singing in a loud voice, to the "Hallelujah Chorus"*) Alopecia! Alopecia! Alopecia. Alopecia. Al-o-o-pecia!

(HARRY *sits in his chair, setting his face into an expression of disinterest.* CHARLIE *prances round him, pointing at the bandages*)

Alopecia! Alopecia! Alopecia. Alopecia. Oh alo-p-pe-cia. Etc. Etc.
(*He collapses, laughing, into his chair*)

HARRY. Thimble of gin and you're up the Monument. I don't know.

CHARLIE. God! For a parade of swans in a lane of diamonds—instead of paper boats in dirty buckets. D'you know, Harry, I haven't one single memory. Did you know? Not a single memory. Never stick. Never stick. My only flash of life is a day at school: there was a real ram of a lad, and his sister. We called her Milky Moe because she was overdeveloped. She was six. And Milky Moe stole my frog.

HARRY. Milky Moe did what?

CHARLIE. Stole my frog, dear. My frog. A-wooing-go and all that. I worshipped that frog. I'll bet there's something deeply psychological if I could but lay my fingers upon it.

HARRY (*rising and picking up the bottle*) I could lend you memories; but you never listen.

CHARLIE. Goldfish bowls! Goldfish bowls, you said; a damn lie! I never mentioned them.

HARRY. Ah, but you said you felt like a fly in a milk bottle. And *I* feel like a fly on a goldfish bowl, d'you see? Sort of walking *outside the world* all day. Worse! I'm worse. (*He puts the bottle on the basin* R) A fly probably knows he can't get his feet wet and enjoys his stroll. I long to wet me feet and haven't the guts to jump in!

CHARLIE (*impressed*) You dig up some interesting rubbish on the quiet, Harry. (*He rises and, taking his glass, moves* L *to the mirror*)

HARRY. Thank you. Oh, I was always the strange one. (*Sitting in his chair*) Unhappy child, I was, Charlie. It was all this "Vive la différence!" hoo-hah. I remember, as a lad at the swimming baths—the women with their bodies all private, on one side; and the men on another side. A funny business, it seemed. I'd look at *my* body; and I'd think there's a woman next door, looking at hers. And I couldn't, you know, get me thoughts untangled.

CHARLIE (*gazing at himself in the mirror*) I might dye my hair, I think. Make me look less evil at the trial.

HARRY. Life's just two great separate piles. You're supposed to whoop from one to the other; and if God's given you enough bounce, Bob's your uncle. If not—you're right in it! I've tried hard, Charlie. Once I wore long scarves; rubbed me hands when anyone mentioned beer; and chuckled in dark brown if they asked "Are you courting?" Till I was thirty-five I did that; then I started getting headaches. Just those two piles; nothing down the middle.

CHARLIE (*still at the mirror*) I have a kindly face in the main.

HARRY. I had a talk with a parson once; you know, a vicar—for advice. But he was more embarrassed than me, Charlie. Couldn't shuffle his face into the right expression. Looked as though he'd just noticed horns on the curate! Made me a cup of tea and told me about his eight children. Eight children, he had!

CHARLIE. Typical! Tells you to put your trust in God: then dashes to the manse for a bunk-up! (*He soothes wrinkles round his eyes, then considers himself*) 'Course, *I* look well in clerical grey. Me best bet, that is, looking hen-pecked and married. By hell—I could take Cassy. (*He swings round*) "This is my daughter, Gentlemen of the Jury"— Your Honour! M'Lud! *Meet my daughter.* That'd shake 'em. Ha! (*Then his triumphant mood fades*) But how'd I tell her in the first place? Going to be a trial saying "How-do" without ploughing straight into a homosexual homily or whatever-it-is.

HARRY. It's a nuisance, the whole thing. (*He rises, puts his glass on the basin* R, *and moves* C) I'm very sorry about it all, Charlie.

CHARLIE. Yes; but, I mean, if she turned out to be a wowzer, Harry. You know, mate: a real lush babe. And I could say *That is mine!* I *made* that!

HARRY. Marvellous, Charlie!

CHARLIE (*moving* L.C) Aw . . .! I should be that lucky, dear! What! I'll bet she's threaded on twine; face like a whippet; and a bosom like two monocles on a monk's bench. (*He flops into his chair*)

(HARRY *moves to him and stands behind, patting his shoulders*)

HARRY. If it's any help, Charlie—I'm frightened, too.

CHARLIE. Thanks. (*Then, as though surprised*) It *is* a help, Harry. A nice help—you breast-fed gnat! (*He shakes his head, then lowers it*) If only—if only it hadn't happened, Harry. If only it hadn't happened. If only I could stare at me shoes—and blur me eyes—and find myself in a different safe moment when I look up . . . (*For several seconds he stares at his shoes*)

(HARRY *keeps patting his shoulders*)

(*Whispers*) It's not happening—not happening. I'm not here . . . (*Then he looks up; but it's the same old moment! He probes his fists deep into his stomach and groans*)

HARRY. They can't do anything if you're innocent, Charlie. And you *are* innocent—aren't you—Charlie!

CHARLIE. Do I have to grovel for you, too? Humiliate myself here as well?

HARRY. No. No, Charlie; but we'll get by somehow.

CHARLIE. I hope so, mate. (*He reaches up and pats Harry's hand*) By God, I hope so.

HARRY. What starts it! (*Moving* R *and picking up the bottle and his glass*) Oogh, it's frustrating! What makes a violinist—a genius—a great lover! They say it's hormones; and I detest the whole damn system, I do! You know—(*moving* C *and pouring two more gins*)—they showed films—in one of those operating shows on television—they showed you moving pictures of the whole reproductive system of a ferret.

CHARLIE. In opposition to the London Palladium, was it?

HARRY. Ha . . . No, it was fascinating, really. All these magni-fied actually moving photographs. And a ferret—or was it a horse?
CHARLIE. Easily mistaken.
HARRY. No, it was a horse, this bit. Fantastic, dear! Actual photographs of a thousand squiggling *things. Carnal things*—squiggling inside this horse . . .!
CHARLIE. Urrrgh, you obscene hag!
HARRY. But it's true, Charlie. *Things! In us!* Oh I hate life. Hate it! Hate the whole dirty business . . .
CHARLIE. Oh belt up, will you! Will you belt up! You twisted umbilicologist! *I'm trying to forget!*

(HARRY *moves* R *and puts the bottle back on the basin*)

My head's corrugated and there's cannon balls rumbling over the ruts. I've enough to worry on the outside without you medicating all over the . . . (*He stops. Then slowly, worriedly*) Harry, you don't think—I mean—I've seen it in the newspapers: "Remanded for a medical report". (*His voice shakes*) Harry, you don't suppose they'll remand me for—f-for anything like that?

(HARRY *moves to him*)

HARRY. No, Charlie. No, no, no, love.
CHARLIE. Remanded for a medical report.
HARRY. Oh, that's a different situation . . .

(CHARLIE *looks small, old and pathetic*)

CHARLIE. Old Charlie, hair stylist and one-time dramatic actor, was this morning rem-m- . . . (*He covers his mouth*)

(*Now* HARRY *clears his throat and puts on a business-like air*)

HARRY. I'll leave you alone, Charlie, when . . .

(*But before Harry can finish his sentence,* CHARLIE *grabs his arm anxiously*)

CHARLIE. No! Guddelpus no! *Not alone.*
HARRY. When Cassy comes, I meant.
CHARLIE. Oh! Oh yes—thanks.
HARRY. And be quite honest, Charlie. Tell her the truth; and ask if she'll come to Court with you. It's your best bet.
CHARLIE. Yes. Yes, it is. (*He surges into fresh optimism*) And per-haps we could sprinkle a few of your mother's knick-knacks around: even down here, as well. You know, everywhere.
HARRY. Knick-knacks, um . . .
CHARLIE. Well, I shan't be seeing my mother until afterwards, or I'd've borrowed her stuff.
HARRY. No, take my mother's.
CHARLIE. Good. Good. Thanks, love. (*He turns his chair to face his mirror*) I might grow a moustache by next Wednesday.

HARRY. Charlie! Why?

CHARLIE. Mm?

HARRY. Why d'you want mother's knick-knacks?

CHARLIE. Um—(*he shrugs*)—oh, you're not connected with the theatre. A dramatic touch.

HARRY. Tell me, Charlie!

CHARLIE. Well—she'll imagine I'm living with some fancy woman instead of . . . (*He stops*)

HARRY. Instead of me.

CHARLIE. It's better than have her wondering things, isn't it! Oh—who cares!

HARRY (*moving above Charlie's chair to the window*) I care! I blasted care! You're making me a—a filthy shadow. Shall I scratch my name off the window, too?

CHARLIE. What're you going up for?

HARRY (*crossing back above Charlie to* C) I'm fed up being hidden and elbowed into shadows to suit you!

CHARLIE. Tragic stint? Tragic stint?

HARRY. The one person in life I'd've liked to meet would be Cassy. She's the one *real* thing—the only *real* thing about you, Charlie.

CHARLIE. It was your own suggestion. "I'll go out", you said.

HARRY. To suit you! By hell! A lifetime of bolstering *you*; feeding *you*; worrying for you. And now you're too damned ashamed to have Cassy meet me—*in my own home*.

CHARLIE. I'll tell you about the time I had digs in Clitheroe . . .

HARRY. When have you ever bolstered *me*? (*Moving below his own chair*) Never! Never once said "Well done" or "Nice work, Harry!"

CHARLIE. Last Monday I said the porridge was nice. I distinctly remember: "Christ, Harry," I said, "this is beautiful porridge".

HARRY. Porridge! When have you ever made me feel big?

CHARLIE. Maybe you're not big, mate! Maybe you're not. (*He regrets this immediately*) I was joking, dear. (*He rises and moves to Harry*)

HARRY (*quietly*) You weren't, Charlie. That's the whole point. Deep down you believe you're better than me. Don't you! Answer me, Charlie.

CHARLIE. Well, I am artistic, aren't I. I mean—I can't help what I feel, can I? (*He moves away* C)

HARRY. Well blast you! You and your whole cruel West End sardonic bunch. You balance your own failures by insulting others. That's why you get at me with your quick wit and ready repartee: you use me as a kind of staircase between flops.

CHARLIE. And up you and your good-will-to-men for a start! What! I should . . . Goddam it, you're standing there, on that very spot, doing exactly what you're accusing me of! Grinding me down as you've done for twenty years.

HARRY. Oh, I'll not have that!

CHARLIE. Not have it! Not have it! *You've got it!*

HARRY. Yes—well—who says *you're* so big? What've you ever done? And anyway, how d'you know she's yours, dear?

CHARLIE. How what? Who? *She? She who?*

(HARRY *regrets now*)

HARRY. Nothing.

CHARLIE. Talking about Cassy, weren't we! Another vicious goose from my ever-loving mate! It's like living on a vampire's pogo stick.

HARRY. Charlie . . .

CHARLIE. She's *mine*; mine, you bastard!

HARRY. Yes. Of course she is.

CHARLIE. God, you're clever! Just slide 'em in, don't you: the little doubt, beautifully cooked, just slipped under me eyeballs to scratch and niggle.

HARRY. Well *she'll* not like you dragging Cassy into it. What if she said . . .

CHARLIE. A lie! A lie!

HARRY (*heatedly*) Maybe; but *I* shouldn't want a daughter dragged through the mud, alibi-ing her father's—lovelife. "No thank you," I'd say. "She's not his!" I'd say. "He's just a bum I married for convenience," I'd say. Any lie I'd tell if I were Cassy's mother.

CHARLIE (*shouting*) Well, you're bloody not—much to your creeping disappointment, Mrs Lactating Harriet Leeds!

(HARRY *shrugs.* CHARLIE *glowers for a few seconds, then plucks his lip thoughtfully*)

It'd be slander, that would. *I* did the asking. *Me!* Real masher in those days, I was. Oogh, I was so beautiful it hurt.

HARRY. Yes, Charlie . . .

CHARLIE. Back line of the chorus, *her.*

HARRY. Yes, I know.

CHARLIE. Snapped me fingers. Snapped me fingers and she was grovelling . . .

HARRY. Charlie—Cassy was premature; it only needs some legal bigwig to uncover . . .

CHARLIE. Bigwig! Bigwig! Where're they trying me, House o' Lords? 'S'only a tiddly Case for God's sake. Local butcher they'll have on the bench; he won't postpone to search Somerset-blasted-House. Cassy's *mine. Mine.* She has my—my eyes—my . . . Anyhow, me and the Old Sow were having it off for years, boy, years!

HARRY (*quietly*) You weren't, Charlie. You weren't.

CHARLIE. You wide-hipped belly-grubber . . .! (*His intended blistering volley stops suddenly. The words choke him. He covers his face; and his voice is low, near to tears*) Did you *have* to bring it up? Could've done without this one. W-wouldn't involve me own daughter, I wouldn't: just a quick idea to keep me going. (*He raises his face; eyes closed, hands clenched*) If only I'd been certain all those years ago. If only I'd been sure, I might never have . . . Oh, if only it hadn't happened. (*To Harry; ferociously*) You! Hope your nipples drop off as well! Dog in the manger? You've got hyenas!

(HARRY *shrugs into his chair.* CHARLIE *strides over, towering above him*)

Oh, I see it now. Anything to whittle me to *your* level. (*Shouting cruelly*) I bet you pray nights: "*Please God make Charlie small like me!*"

(HARRY *leans forward, his head in his hands*)

HARRY. Oh—I feel dizzy, I think.

CHARLIE. Here we go! The "oh-me-heart" stint; the "coughing-me-last-hours" stint! Ask yourself honestly: are you or are you not happy when there's no excitement in my letters—no television work—nothing in me pocket—and nowhere to go except this hairy-aired brilliantine fleapit? Well?

HARRY (*leaning his head back*) I suppose I have been jealous sometimes but . . .

CHARLIE. She admits it! Right out? (*He moves to the window, and turns*) I suppose you realize you copy me? You copy me, you're so envious.

HARRY. When you live close to someone, you can't . . . (*He shakes his head; he is unable to finish*)

CHARLIE. Why don't you fight back? What're you so silent for? On our pale and wan stint, are we?

HARRY. Have you ever wondered if I'm really here?

CHARLIE. Oh guddelpus! That's the second time today! *You're there!* Slap bang *there!*

HARRY. Like your agent, Archy Selder?

CHARLIE (*moving below his chair*) You what!

HARRY. You've no agent, Charlie.

CHARLIE. Ha! (*Blustering*) Oh rich! Oh . . .

HARRY. Archy—spelled with a Y. Usually it's spelled I E. Isn't it?

(CHARLIE *is still and apprehensive. He says nothing.* HARRY *takes a paper from his pocket*)

And d'you remember those postcards when you were away? When you used to write about the great play you were starring in; and your co-star Sherry Clade?

CHARLIE. A great voice! Sherry Clade could reach a top C above . . .

HARRY. And your famous impresario D'Arcy Relshe; and the society woman who worshipped you, Sherly Drace? And Chard Seerly and so on?

CHARLIE. Doing a biography, are you? Biography?

HARRY. I jotted all those names on a paper. I got to thinking, you see. What a funny name, I thought—Chard Seerly; and Archy Selder with a Y; and D'Arcy Relshe! (*He rises to face Charlie*) They all spell Charles Dyer. *They're all you*, Charlie! You've never mentioned anyone who isn't an anagram of Charles Dyer.

(CHARLIE *sits in his chair and swings to face the mirror* L. HARRY *tosses the paper in front of him.* CHARLIE *clears his throat*)

CHARLIE. Bit dumb if you've only just found out.

HARRY. I've known for years.

CHARLIE. I once started a play, Harry. Never finished it—thought it might be an idea to have everyone's names the same as mine.

HARRY. Charlie, what—I've always been frightened—what were you really doing? During those two years?

CHARLIE. I-I was, um—selling encyclopedias.

HARRY (*in relief*) Is that all?

CHARLIE. I need excitement, Harry. Haven't your guts to be ordinary, Harry. Hate being ordinary.

HARRY. Yes—but I want to know, Charlie. Was there anything else?

CHARLIE. Um—I was on me own, Harry, d'you see. You kicked me out and . . .

HARRY. You walked out.

CHARLIE. Well, anyway, I landed in doss houses some nights. Oh, horrid dumps I slept in. Wasn't much commission on 'cyclopedias; and I like a good laundry for me shirts, dear. And one day, I thought —What! I might as well be in— (*he pushes these words through his pride*) —be in jail. Ha ha.

HARRY. Oh my God!

CHARLIE. I'm glad it's out, Harry. Been choking me—ever since the summons. Had to tell someone.

HARRY (*wearily*) It'll be on your records.

CHARLIE (*with a flash of spirit*) Think you're telling me? Do you? Why d'you think me head's been corrugated all night?

HARRY. What was the charge?

CHARLIE. I got thirty days . . .

HARRY. The charge, Charlie! As though I didn't know . . .

CHARLIE. I did nothing, Harry. It was a pub near this air force base. Youngsters marching with their proud chests—and I was kipping in this cellar at four bob a night—old meths drinkers belching in me ears. And you know I enjoy a bit of comfort. I—I just asked a lad if I could come back to camp with him.

(HARRY *covers his face and groans.*

CHARLIE. (*Vehemently*) There but for the grace of God, Harry! There but for the Grace! By hell, if ever I finish me great play, I'll name the villain after meself: to prove I've a spit o' faith in humanity; to show there's one living Twit with enough compassion not to label

others 'you people' or 'them' or 'those'; to prove I've enough
humility to travel under any label—any label—without shame.
(*Tiny voice*) I never do anything, you know that, Harry. God's
Truth, I never do anything. I just like clean, new people; fresh and
young. Like being *near* them.

(*Now we realize, gradually, that* HARRY *is the stronger of the partner-
ship. It is* CHARLIE *who is the weak one*)

HARRY. You met him in a pub.

CHARLIE. Yes. Well, I'd kept 'em laughing. Kept 'em in stitches
with me tales, Harry. I've a vibrant personality. I'm an old pro-
They'd never heard some of my songs. But—I was all alone at closing
time.

HARRY. This finishes us! (*He moves down* R)

CHARLIE. Aw—it's ten years ago.

HARRY. You promised. *Promised.* Said you'd only drink at home.
Swore on my mother's upstairs Bible.

CHARLIE. We'd had a row, hadn't we! Your Bible didn't count
on the two years.

HARRY. So hundreds of policemen surrounded the air force base
and drummed lies in the Judge's ear.

CHARLIE (*nodding*) Ninety days—for nothing.

HARRY. Two years was your sentence, Charlie, wasn't it! Two
years.

CHARLIE (*nodding*) Nearly—nearly. Um, they let you out early,
d'you see. If you're good.

HARRY (*flaming into anger*) D'you never consider anyone? Never
think of *my* shame? Staying with you! People pointing at us—at the
two weirdies, Harry and Charlie. *And there's nothing wrong with me.*
There's nothing wrong, and I have to suffer the strain because of *you.*

CHARLIE. You what! I should rub a dub. I mean, you're hardly
Ghenkis Khan, are you, dear! So don't waft your feathers too high—
we'll see your corsets.

(HARRY *moves up* C *and rests his head against the wall*)

HARRY. Oh, I feel wretched. What with you, and the gin, and
being up all night. This finishes us. Finished! I warned you. Warned
you and warned you.

(*There is a pause*)

CHARLIE. And to think my father was a parson! Although they
say he was odd, too. Left me mother—he wrote "You wear it!" on
his collar and flung it in the hall. Very religious man, he was. Very
religious. A Muswell Hill Adventist or something, he was.

(HARRY, *on a sudden thought, takes a pencil from the shelf* C, *picks up
the folded newspaper and writes on it*)

HARRY (*muttering*) Ed Chryslar . . . (*He ticks off the letters, then
looks up*) So you were sitting on Ed Chryslar's knee for a gag!

CHARLIE. I know. I know. Ed Chryslar spells me own name, as well.

(HARRY *moves to him*)

(*Quickly, before Harry can start on questions*) No use asking me, Harry, because I can't remember.

(HARRY *sits in his chair*)

Drunk. Drunk. When I came to, they were dragging me out of the Club; said I was masquerading—masquerading as a w-woman. Young copper, scuffing me. Fell on me knees, I did; scraped them all. I was clutching his legs; everyone watching. "Please, *please*," I said, "you'll ruin my life, son." I'd've been in the Maria except for this nice Inspector. "Up you get, Dad," he said—calling me "dad" now! But he told this young copper. What! "Can't you see this is a gentleman," he said.

HARRY. Did he hell!

CHARLIE (*after a pause*) He said something quite nice.

HARRY. Yeah—what?

CHARLIE. "Don't be greedy," he said. "Send the poor old bugger home." (*He sits nodding his head for a moment or two in silence*) "He might do himself in or something." the young copper said. And the Inspector said: "Save time if he did." Yes, I've known three who did, Harry. Three who did. A problem, it is. Such a problem. Ruined me marriage, you know.

HARRY. Oh, it was the Problem, was it? I see.

CHARLIE (*with a shrug*) May as well take all offences into consideration—Ladies and Gentlemen of the Jury. She was a good person, really, the Old Sow. A good old sow, she was. If I'd had one spot of tact . . . What! I've as much tact as a stallion's buttock.

HARRY. And I'm twice as ugly.

CHARLIE. I know she was only after a baby. I know that. It was me body, mate! Me health and beauty. But um, I wish I was back with her. (*He shakes his head*) Wish she hadn't kicked me out.

HARRY. Do you! Do you really! Oh well. (*He busies himself. He rises, leaving the newspaper and pencil by his chair, moves to the window and looks out*)

(*It is well into morning—it could be six o'clock or later.* HARRY *pushes up a large electric switch—perhaps the neon sign or burglar alarm. Then he moves* R *and picks up the towel from the basin*)

(*As he moves*) Once, when Mother needed a hairnet, I popped to the chemist on the corner; and—you know—I didn't like asking for it.

CHARLIE. So I should damn well think! A barber asking a chemist for an 'airnet! Sounds like a code word.

HARRY. Well, we'd sold out. Anyway, I said it was for my wife. And ever after they kept asking: "How's your wife?" Oh, I loved it. Loved having a wife.

(*We hear a milkman's shout off; bottles rattle on the step*)

It made me belong; like a parson in swim trunks getting a slap on the back.

CHARLIE. You're not twisted: you're hexagonal.

(HARRY *switches off the room lights up* C, *then picks up the towel from the basin* L *and moves to the stock room door*)

HARRY. But now I'm nothing again. (*He turns*) Have you ever thought about my name, Charlie?

CHARLIE. Bluddyell! What're you flogging this line for? On the psycho stint, are we? Psycho stint? Your name's Harry Leeds, mate. Very pretty.

HARRY. It spells Charles Dyer.

(HARRY *exits into the stock room.* CHARLIE *sits quite still for a second or so, then rises to pick up the newspaper and pencil and sits scribbling on it, muttering*)

CHARLIE. H-A-R-R-Y—Harry. L-E-E . . . (*Having written the name, he crosses out the letters one by one*)

(HARRY *enters from the stock room with a sweeping brush*)

HARRY. Fantastic, isn't it!

CHARLIE. There's no C.

HARRY. C for Chris, my middle name. You know I always sign myself Harry C. Leeds. (*He moves above his chair*)

CHARLIE (*rising*) Oogh, *you must be joking!* (*He backs away* L) See me inventing you! Pull the other one!

HARRY (*moving* C) Strange though, eh?

(CHARLIE *backs away from him again*)

CHARLIE. I'm getting out! Out, mate! By God, you're right we're finished. I'm getting out before little goblins start running up me arm. (*He runs to the lobby, brings on a suitcase, puts it on the arms of his chair, and starts collecting his personal combs, brushes, clippers, scissors and things from the cupboard and shelf down* L *and putting them into it*) I'll go to a bloody nunnery! (*Then he pours the contents of his mother's souvenir box into the case*) I only make beautiful people. Beautiful people, I make. Like nice fresh sweet-smelling things, I do. You! You're shrivelled and ordinary, mate! Accuse me of creating you! What! I'm no impressionist. I'd have someone with black curls. Black curls I'd have. I should rub a dub. (*He stops, breathless, and looks at Harry*) Nothing to say? Nothing to say, then? I'm going, you know. Walking out that door.

(HARRY *moves up* R *to sweep stray clippings into a pile on the floor*)

HARRY. Terrible terrible thing—not to be liked; not to be even necessary. If a great big nozzle sucked me into oblivion, there isn't a clock'd stop ticking.

CHARLIE. Got to make yourself not care, mate: like me.

HARRY. Trouble with our sort, you're never left with anyone. 'S' an impossibility. It's an empty room when whatever friends you've got go first.

CHARLIE. Twenty years I've stuck by you.

HARRY. Well, it's been warm; and I've taught you a trade, Charlie.

CHARLIE. Oh, I'll put that in "Spotlight". Leading Character Actor. Shakespeare a Speciality. Able to Drive—And Trim Nostrils! (*He pushes his case to the floor with a thud*)

(HARRY, *having swept the dusty fluff on to a newspaper, empties it into the waste bin up* R. *Then he takes his brush to the stock room door*)

HARRY. It's not one-sided, Charlie: because I need somebody all my own. And after all, I can't see a "little me" in *you*, Charlie. Can't watch *you* growing up. A shame, it is: we could've walked through the years together. Blame's on both sides, I suppose.

(HARRY *exits into the stock room, closing the door. After a second,* CHARLIE *moves to the stock room door. He calls quietly*)

CHARLIE. Harry! Harry? Aren't you going to wait for me, then? Harry? Oh, suit yourself. (*There is no reply. He kicks the door and moves to the gin bottle. It is empty*) Dry as a camel's chamber pot! (*He tosses the bottle into the waste bin, then looks about him, scratching his neck and licking his lips*) Hair restorer! I'll have a tot of that. (*He shouts at the stock room*) And maybe I'll die; then you'll be sorry! (*He rummages in the cupboard down* L *and produces a bottle of hair restorer. Shouting*) I'm having hair restorer! D'you hear—you ramshackle old queen! (*To himself*) But he's not. He's nice and ordinary; that's the trouble. (*He clenches his teeth*) God, I wish I could say straight out: "Harry, you're a beautiful old stick, love." Why can't I say it? Why can't I say: "Please Harry, keep me room warm for when I come out of jail"? (*He turns to face the stock room. Firmly, he calls*) Harry, Harry! will you . . . (*But he cannot make his lips finish the sentence. Instead, he puts the bottle to his lips and gulps the hair restorer—which he immediately spits into the basin* L) Uurrgh! I'll die *next* week, I think. (*For a while he leans on the wash basin, peering at himself in the mirror*) Harry C. Leeds. Harry C. Leeds. Fantastic! I never planned that one! Don't say I'm seeing 'em as well! (*He swings away from the mirror and shouts*) Of course you're there! I wouldn't invent a shrivelled mirage like you, mate! (*To himself*) Oh no! I'd have someone with black curls and slim hips. (*He shouts*) You there, mate! You're horrible and concrete! (*He moves to the stock room door; bangs on it*) D'you hear? Harry? Harry! (*He tries the door knob. Seemingly it is locked*) Harry, what're you doing? (*He bangs on the door*) Damn fool—locking the door! Harry! You all right, Harry? Harry! Harry, what've you done?

(CHARLIE'S *shouting and banging becomes frantic. He pushes against the door. It begins to open—slowly, as though something heavy were lying on the other side. Eventually,* CHARLIE *forces his way in.* HARRY *is lying on the floor.* CHARLIE *steps over him and out of sight. We hear him coughing—then the sound of breaking glass.* CHARLIE *returns in view and drags Harry into the shop, below the chair* RC)

(*In tears*) Fool! Bloody fool! (*He applies artificial respiration*) Not alone, Harry. Don't leave me. Not alone—not alone—not alone, Harry. (*He listens at Harry's chest, then tries more hopefully*) You bastard. Can't be so bad! Holding out for the kiss of life, mate? What! I should rub a dub. Back, boy. Come back. Harry, come back, love!

(HARRY *starts coughing. He pushes Charlie away and sits up*)

HARRY. What—what're you—what're you doing?

(CHARLIE *sits back, panting from his exertions*)

CHARLIE. Oh lovely! Yes! I've only strained me heart saving you. I could kill you for this.

HARRY. Oogh, I'm feeling better.

CHARLIE. Mean slut-faced puff, trying to leave me! You'll never live this down, dear. Never. Why d'you do it?

HARRY. I did nothing, Charlie.

CHARLIE. I'll never feel safe with you. Spend me life watching you.

HARRY. Just—sort of red came upwards across my eyes. And d'you know, Charlie: I heard my own bang as I hit the floor.

(CHARLIE *rises and moves to the stock room*)

CHARLIE. Squatting there with your small talk. I might've had the coppers in. Coppers, mate!

HARRY. What coppers?

CHARLIE (*closing the stock room door*) What coppers? *What coppers?* (*He stops at a sudden thought. Opening the door again, he sniffs the atmosphere*)

HARRY. No need for sniffing. I checked the jet.

CHARLIE. It's in! (*Accusingly*) That flame's still in. (*He moves above his chair*)

HARRY. 'Course it is. (*He rises, brushing himself down*)

CHARLIE. But—but I've just smashed that window.

HARRY. Silly bee! Wasn't it funny, though: touch of blood pressure, I bet; I had it once before, remember?

(HARRY *moves to the stock room.* CHARLIE *steadies himself against his chair, leaning over it*)

I'm back to myself now. All fine . . . (*He notices Charlie*) Here! What is it, dear? (*He hurries down* c)

CHARLIE. The shock, mate! The shock. Phewsh! (*He slides to his knees* R *of his chair*)

HARRY (*realizing*) Charlie! *You thought*—oh hell!

CHARLIE. Yes—*that's* where I thought you'd gone. Disappointed now.

HARRY (*kneeling beside him*) Bit of a shock, was it?

CHARLIE (*nodding*) I thought, um—thought I was on me own, Harry. And um, I think you're . . . (*He tries again*) I think you're— (*and in a whisper*) —a beautiful old stick.

(*But* HARRY *does not hear Charlie's whisper*)

HARRY. Pardon? I couldn't hear, Charlie.

CHARLIE. Oh belt up, and give me breathing space. (*He elbows Harry away*)

HARRY (*rising*) Very well, Charlie. You take things easy, eh? Here, shall we close today?

CHARLIE. Could do.

HARRY. Have the day off, eh? Right you are.

(HARRY *exits into the stock room*)

CHARLIE (*to himself*) Too old for this lark! God, what would I have done? Nowhere to go! And what about *him*? (*He looks upwards*) There! I thought about him, God. I did think about *him*, God-mate. (*He closes his eyes, speaking fervently; and—even though, in seconds hence, he'll be back to the same old Charlie—in this one moment, Charlie believes in God; and by God he prays!*) Oh God, make me remember this. Please God, just help me at the Assizes, as well; and I'll never think another foul thing. And I'll make Harry diet and see a doctor. And may Mum drop dead and everyone leave me alone if I don't remember this lesson. *I will. I will.* Please Jesus, make me remember how lonely people are; little cripples and little blind folks. Amen.

HARRY (*off*) Charlie, don't be cruel!

(CHARLIE *is startled. He opens his eyes fearfully, thinking God has spoken*)

CHARLIE. Who said that!

(HARRY *enters, wearing a thin, bad wig. He moves* L *of his chair and waits apprehensively, as* CHARLIE *turns to look.* CHARLIE *rises from his knees. He tries hard—but cannot enthuse; instead, he seems cowed and subdued*)

Ah! It's quite nice. Very nice, Harry.

HARRY. Well, I warned you, didn't I?

CHARLIE. No! It's nice. It's um—didn't they have any other colours?

HARRY. My hair *was* black. Curly black. Thick black curls, I had.

CHARLIE. Oh yes. Yes, I know. I know.

HARRY. You don't like it. Knew you wouldn't. Said so.

CHARLIE. I do. I do, Harry.

HARRY. Oh, I hate you like this—all subdued and holy. Are you staying for ever like this?

CHARLIE. Well . . . (*He shrugs*)

HARRY. I'd rather you said one of your cruel thrusts. Go on, Charlie. Get it off your chest.

CHARLIE. The wig's fine, dear. Fine. (*He moves away* LC)

HARRY (*following Charlie and holding his arm*) Charlie! Charlie, I don't mind. Tell me the truth. Be yourself!

(CHARLIE *stops and looks over his shoulder at Harry's head. That old evil relish glimmers—*)

CHARLIE. Where're you . . . (*He stops*)

HARRY. Don't stop, Charlie! Straight out!

CHARLIE. Where're you going to keep it at night—in a cage?

HARRY. Yes, that's you! That's my old You. Go on! More. Tell me more.

CHARLIE. Well—it looks like you've spat ink on a hot boiled egg!

(*But this is too much for Harry*)

HARRY. Oh, you bastard! You're horrid and vicious.

CHARLIE. You asked me! Asked me!

HARRY. You and your pretty hair! I hope it erupts from your scalp. Erupts and erupts—until the shop's an overgrown church hassock with taps; and you in the middle, clawing for life. Hair in your eyes, through your ears, and up your bloody jumper! (*He flops into his chair*)

(CHARLIE *moves to him*)

CHARLIE. You going to wear that when you meet Cassy?

HARRY. Meet her?

CHARLIE. Might as well. Anything for peace. (*He walks round Harry, surveying the wig*) Could be worse. Pleasantly surprised, I am. It sort of grows on you. Sorry, Harry. (*He moves* L *and considers himself in the mirror. A night has passed, and his chin is shadowed again*)

(*We hear creaking on the staircase. They look upwards.* HARRY *rises and rushes to listen; but* CHARLIE *just rubs his chin at the mirror and murmurs—*)

CHARLIE. Ta-ta, Sexy!

Now CHARLIE *sighs; sits in his chair.* HARRY *bustles to his record-player and puts on the "Hallelujah Chorus"; then he goes to his basin* R, *takes his little bowl and soap, and begins lathering the brush, as—*

the CURTAIN *falls*

AUTHOR'S NOTE

During the writing I began to feel, I think, that Charlie is alone. Nobody else. This should not affect the Reader's sense of reality, because I believed in my characters; loved them; they were very, very real inside me. Yet only one person wrote them! So it *could* be just Charlie in a grubby little barber shop. No Harry! And perhaps that Case, that Incident, exists only in Charlie's mind. Isn't the Chief Constable of the Summons an anagram, as well? Or maybe it's just Harry; and no Charlie! But whatever the truth, this is a story of deep loneliness. . . .

FURNITURE AND PROPERTY LIST

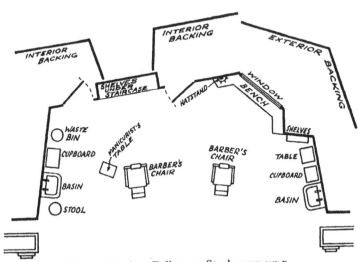

Type A Setting. Full stage. Stock room up R.
(As in American and European productions)

ACT I

SCENE 1

On stage: 2 barber's chairs (RC and LC) *On LC chair:* sheet (for Charlie),
razor (for Harry)

Padded bench (L) *On upstage end:* portable record player with
record on turntable. *On downstage end:* magazines, newspaper
folded open at crossword.

Attached to upstage end: hat-stand with Charlie's white coat and
Harry's cardigan on it

Manicurist's table (RC) *On it:* manicuring implements

Stool (*down R*)

Table (L) *On it:* electric kettle, cups, saucers, teaspoons, 2 mugs,
knives

2 basins (down R and down L) *On them:* razors, bowls, shaving
brushes and soap, scissors, combs (above them) mirrors

2 cupboards (connected with basins). *In L cupboard:* bottle of gin,
dictionary, antique deed box containing flower in pressed
book, lock of hair and various mementoes, bottle of hair

restorer, various hairdressing implements. *In* R *cupboard:* bottle
of surgical spirit, various hairdressing implements

Shelves (under stairwell up c) *On top:* cash register, pads, pencils,
newspapers. *On shelves:* toilet preparations, bottles, cotton
wool

Waste bin (above R basin)

Shelves (on wall down L) *On them:* tins of tea and sugar, wrapped
marzipan roll, teapot, milk bottle, roll of sticking tape, bar of
chocolate, tumblers

On stock room door: framed certificate

On walls: photographs of male hair-styles, calendar, posters,
horse-shoes

On floor up R*:* hair clippings and fluff

Window curtains

Off stage:	Hot towel (HARRY)
	Hot towel (CHARLIE)
	Card (POLICEMAN)
	Summons (POLICEMAN)
Personal:	CHARLIE: letter
	HARRY: spectacles

SCENE 2

Set:	Shawl for Charlie on his chair
Off stage:	Packet of aspirins (HARRY)

ACT II

Off stage:	Charlie's dressing gown (HARRY)
	Sweeping brush (HARRY)
	Suitcase (CHARLIE)
	Wig (HARRY)
Personal:	HARRY: paper

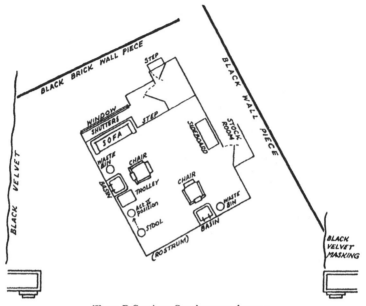

Type B Setting. Stock room down L.
(As used by Royal Shakespeare Company)

LIGHTING PLOT

Property fitting required: globe pendants
    INTERIOR. A barber's shop. The same scene throughout
    THE APPARENT SOURCES OF LIGHT are: by day, a window L; by night,
      pendants
    THE MAIN ACTING AREAS are R, up RC, up and down C, LC, down L

ACT I. SCENE 1. Night

To open: Fittings on

No cues

SCENE 2. Night

To open: As Act I Scene 1

No cues

ACT II. Early morning

To open: Fittings off. Effect of dawn outside window

Cue 1	On CURTAIN up *Start slow fade up to daylight*	(Page 26)
Cue 2	HARRY switches on lights *Snap on pendants. Note: Continue Cue 1 throughout Act*	(Page 26)
Cue 3	HARRY switches off lights *Snap off pendants*	(Page 41)

EFFECTS PLOT

ACT I

SCENE 1

Lightning Source UK Ltd.
Milton Keynes UK
UKOW06f1144250815

257488UK00013B/171/P